D0628128

HEALING YOUR GRIEF
WHEN DISASTER STRIKES

Also by Alan Wolfelt:

*Healing Your Traumatized Heart:
100 Practical Ideas After Someone You
Love Dies a Sudden, Violent Death*

*Healing a Friend's Grieving Heart:
100 Practical Ideas for Helping Someone
You Love Through Loss*

*Creating Meaningful Funeral Ceremonies:
A Guide for Families*

*Healing the Adult Child's Grieving Heart:
100 Practical Ideas After Your Parent Dies*

*The Journey Through Grief:
Reflections on Healing*

*Loving from the Outside In,
Mourning from the Inside Out*

*Understanding Your Grief:
Ten Essential Touchstones for Finding
Hope and Healing Your Heart*

The Wilderness of Grief: Finding Your Way

Companion Press is dedicated to the education and support of both the bereaved and bereavement caregivers. We believe that those who companion the bereaved by walking with them as they journey in grief have a wondrous opportunity: to help others embrace and grow through grief—and to lead fuller, more deeply-lived lives themselves because of this important ministry.

Companion
P R E S S

For a complete catalog and ordering information, visit:

Companion Press
The Center for Loss and Life Transition
3735 Broken Bow Road
Fort Collins, CO 80526
(970) 226-6050
www.centerforloss.com

HEALING YOUR GRIEF
WHEN DISASTER STRIKES

•

100 Practical Ideas for Coping
After a Tornado, Hurricane,
Flood, Earthquake, Wildfire, or
Other Natural Disaster

•

ALAN D. WOLFELT, PH.D.

Companion
PRESS

Fort Collins, Colorado
An imprint of the Center for Loss and Life Transition

Companion Press is an imprint of the
Center for Loss and Life Transition,
3735 Broken Bow Road, Fort Collins, Colorado 80526
970-226-6050
www.centerforloss.com

Companion Press books may be purchased in bulk for sales promotions, premiums or fundraisers. Please contact the publisher at the above address for more information.

Printed in the United States of America

18 17 16 15 14   5 4 3 2 1

ISBN: 978-1-61722-209-2

In Gratitude

A heartfelt thank you to funeral directors Chad Vice and James Beasley for inspiring me to write this book. I met with them shortly after the 2013 Moore, Oklahoma, tornado. As I attempted to honor the stories of love and loss they shared with me, I realized that a resource like this was needed to help families impacted by natural disasters.

Contents

INTRODUCTION

I live on the western edge of Fort Collins, Colorado, on the first foothill of the beautiful Rocky Mountains. To the east lies the jewel that is Fort Collins; to the west rise up ever-higher foothills and, in the distance, majestic mountain peaks.

I feel lucky to live in such a beautiful and sacred place. In recent years, there have also been several times when my family and I have felt anxious, afraid, and even traumatized. Raging, uncontrollable forest fires have come much too close for comfort. Twice we have been evacuated, forced to helplessly watch from afar as the hungry infernos indiscriminately devoured acre upon acre and home upon home. Fortunately for us, though the wildfires have come close, they have so far spared our home.

Unfortunately for us, a different kind of fire—one caused by the incorrect installation of a hot water heater—gutted our home in 2009. Smoke suddenly began rising from the area of our furnace room one early afternoon in December, and within minutes, much of our home's interior was engulfed in flames. Firefighters were able to save the exterior walls, but almost everything inside was a total loss. We had to move out and live in a succession of rental homes for a full year. Most of our belongings were either burned or destroyed by smoke damage. Though no one was injured, this was indeed a disastrous time for our family, and even recounting it today stirs up embers of trauma and loss.

So if you have experienced a natural disaster, I understand something of your pain. I have also been a grief counselor and educator for more than thirty years, and in that time the thousands of mourners I have companioned, the thousands of bereavement caregivers I have had the privilege to know, and my own personal experiences with grief and loss have taught me that no matter its specific cause, grief is a natural and necessary process after loss of any kind.

How common are natural disasters?

When you are personally touched by a local disaster or affected by a large-scale disaster (such as Hurricane Sandy), it can seem that natural disasters are happening everywhere, all the time. Indeed, they are ubiquitous.

According to Prevention Web (preventionweb.net), there were 640 natural disasters in the United States in the twenty-year period from 1980 to 2010. The vast majority of these—392—were storms (hurricanes and tornados), followed by floods, wildfires, earthquakes, and extreme temperatures. More than 12,000 people were killed. Nearly 27 million people were affected.

The United Nations International Strategy for Disaster Reduction says that more than 226 million people globally are affected by natural disasters each year. Earthquakes and droughts kill the most people, while floods and storms affect the most people.

At the time of this writing, recent natural disasters have included Super Typhoon Haiyan, which flattened the Philippines; a category 5 tornado that reduced Moore, Oklahoma, to rubble; and numerous wildfires in Colorado and California, to name just a few.

Of course, I don't provide these wide-scale statistics to diminish the importance of your very personal experience. No matter how common something is, when it happens to you, you experience the loss uniquely and intimately. That fact is foremost in my mind as I write this book. However, it may help you to realize that there are thousands and sometimes millions of others on planet Earth at any given time who understand your journey. Through the miracle of the internet, you can connect with them through online forums, websites, Facebook, and other social media. Reaching out to comfort and be comforted by others who have experienced a natural disaster similar to the one that affected you (or by the same natural disaster that affected you) will help all of you.

Yes, you are grieving

The purpose of this book is to help you understand, embrace, and heal from your many thoughts and feelings after a natural disaster. You see, even if your home, your belongings, and your loved ones were spared, if your life has been touched by a tornado, hurricane, flood, earthquake, fire, drought, or other natural disaster, you are experiencing grief. You might not think of what you're going through as grief because you might associate grief primarily with death, but whenever you experience loss, you grieve.

You have lost your sense of safety. You have lost trust in your surroundings and perhaps in your community's emergency response systems. You may have lost community assets you treasured or relied on, such as roads, parks, bridges, shops, restaurants, etc. You are probably wrestling with why, philosophically speaking, natural disasters happen. You may have personally lost property and even human life.

In one way or many, you have experienced loss as a result of a natural disaster. This means that all of the difficult thoughts and feelings roiling around inside you in the aftermath of the disaster are what we call grief. You are grieving.

What's more, all of the losses that result from natural disasters are caused by nature—a faceless, violent, and random force. Your grief will be shaped by the brutality and seeming senselessness of "acts of God." And speaking of God, you may well be struggling to understand where He is, or is not, in all of this. This too is normal.

If someone you know was killed in the natural disaster

First, I am so sorry for your loss. Death is always hard, but death caused by sudden, violent circumstances is especially painful and challenging. I wrote this book primarily for the millions of people each year who live through or are affected by tornadoes, hurricanes, floods, earthquakes, fires, and other natural disasters. Thanks to current weather forecasting, warning systems, and communications technologies, fewer and fewer people today are killed in these disasters.

But if you are among those touched by natural-disaster-caused deaths in your family, your neighborhood, or your community, you have special needs that are not specifically focused on in this little book. First, I encourage you to seek the support of a professional counselor, a community caregiver such as a minister, and/or a support group. Your grief will be naturally complicated by the cause of death, and you owe it to yourself and your loved ones to get the help you need. And second, I recommend that in addition to this text, you also read my book entitled *Healing Your Traumatized Heart: 100 Practical Ideas After Someone You Love Dies a Sudden, Violent Death*. Together, these two resources will help you understand and embrace your unique grief journey.

The good news

The good news is that grief can be integrated into your life. You can learn to not only cope, but heal. The 100 Ideas in this book will help you understand the basic principles of grief and mourning, especially as they apply to grief caused by a natural disaster. Each idea includes a *carpe diem*, which means "seize the day." The carpe diems are things you can do today, right this minute, to actively integrate your grief.

We humans are a resilient species. We have lived through natural disasters of all kinds for millennia and, despite the vagaries of weather, have continued to progress socially, politically, and technically. But we have not learned to control Mother Nature. Perhaps we never will. And so ultimately, it is this lack of control that we must learn to cope with and even embrace when we are affected by natural disaster.

God bless you. I hope we meet one day.

1.

UNDERSTAND WHAT IT MEANS TO BE "TRAUMATIZED"

"I think anyone whose life has been turned upside down by a disaster has been traumatized."

— Nicol Andrews

- You've been traumatized by a natural disaster. The word "traumatize" comes from the Greek words meaning "wound" and "pierce." You have experienced, witnessed, and/or been touched by a powerful and violent act of nature, and your mind and soul have been wounded by the devastation.

- In this sense, the word "trauma" also refers to intense feelings of shock, fear, anxiety, and helplessness surrounding the event. Trauma is caused by events of such intensity or magnitude of horror or destruction that they would overwhelm any human being's capacity to cope.

- Sudden and violent natural disasters create a kind of psychic injury. Those who experience them are almost always left with frightening and often intrusive thoughts about the event itself as well as its aftermath. Your grief may naturally be complicated by the traumatic nature of the event.

- Remember—your grief is a normal response to an abnormal event.

CARPE DIEM
If you have been having frightening or intrusive thoughts about the natural disaster, share them with someone else today.

4.

UNDERSTAND THAT GRIEF FOLLOWING TRAUMA CAN BE PARTICULARLY DIFFICULT

"Just as the body goes into shock after a physical trauma, so does the human psyche go into shock after the impact of a major loss."
— Anne Grant

- Not only have you and your community suffered a significant loss, but the experience was sudden and violent. The traumatic nature of the disaster will likely make your grief journey especially painful.

- As we've said, grief is the collection of thoughts and feelings you have on the inside after a loss. This includes the thoughts and feelings you have about the day(s) of the disaster itself. Because the disaster was sudden and violent, this aspect of your grief may consume most of your energies, especially in the early weeks and months following the disaster.

- Even much later, after you've come to terms with the experience itself, it will always be a significant part of your grief.

- Remember that just as your feelings of grief need to be expressed, so do your feelings of trauma. Your trauma is part of your grief and also needs to be mourned.

- Keep in mind that "healing" your trauma loss and "curing" your trauma loss are two different concepts. Healing is an active emotional and spiritual process in which you seek to be whole again. Curing is a medical term that implies that someone or something outside of you rids you of your grief. Your grief cannot be "cured"; it will always live inside you.

CARPE DIEM
Find a trusted friend with whom to discuss the difference between "healing" and "curing."

5.

ALLOW FOR NUMBNESS

"Whenever an earthquake or tsunami takes thousands
of innocent lives, a shocked world talks of little else."
— Anne M. Mulcahy

- Feelings of shock, numbness, and disbelief are nature's way of temporarily protecting us from the full reality of a sudden, violent experience. They help us survive our early grief.

- We often think, "I will wake up and this will not have happened." Mourning can feel like being in a dream.

- Your emotions need time to catch up with what your mind has experienced or been told.

- Even after you have moved beyond these initial feelings of shock and disbelief, don't be surprised if they re-emerge. Holidays, anniversaries, and other significant occasions often trigger these normal and necessary feelings.

- Trauma loss often goes beyond what we consider "normal" shock. In fact, you may experience what is called "psychic numbing"—the deadening or shutting off of emotions. Your sense that "this isn't happening to me" may persist for months, sometimes even years. Don't set rigid expectations for yourself and your ability to function "normally" in the world around you.

- Think of shock and numbness as a bandage that your psyche has placed over your wound. The bandage protects the wound until it has become less open and raw. Only after healing has begun and a scab forms can the bandage be removed and the wound openly exposed to the world.

CARPE DIEM

If you're feeling numb, cancel any commitments that require concentration and decision-making. Allow yourself time to regroup.

6.

CONSIDER YOURSELF IN "EMOTIONAL INTENSIVE CARE"

"When you've experienced a disaster, you'll likely be overwhelmed with everything you'll have to deal with in rebuilding your life."

— Lynn Lawrance

• Something catastrophic has happened. Something assaulting to the very core of your being. Something excruciatingly painful.

• Your spirit has been deeply injured. Just as your body could not recover immediately after a serious injury, neither can your psyche.

• Imagine that you've suffered a severe physical injury and are in your hospital's intensive care unit. Your friends and family surround you with their presence and love. The medical staff attends to you constantly. Your body rests and recovers.

• This is the kind of care you need and deserve right now. The blow you have suffered is no less devastating than this imagined physical injury. Allow others to take care of you. Ask for help. Get as much rest as possible. Take time off work. Let household chores slide. In the early weeks and months after the disaster, don't expect—indeed, don't try—to carry on with your normal routine.

• If your home was damaged by the disaster and you have no choice but to complete insurance and/or Federal Emergency Management Administration (FEMA) paperwork and begin the draining process of relocating and rebuilding, ask for help. Ask a friend or family member who was not affected by the disaster but who is good at administrative tasks to help you with the process.

CARPE DIEM

Close your eyes and imagine yourself in "emotional intensive care." Where are you? What kind of care are you receiving? From whom? Arrange a weekend or a week of the emotional and spiritual intensive care you most need.

7.

INVENTORY YOUR LOSSES

"You really don't feel disasters like these until it hits home."
— Charles Scott

• Natural disasters subject us to loss of many kinds. You may have lost your home. You may have lost some or all of your belongings. You may even have experienced the loss of someone close to you.

• Yet even when your home, your belongings, and the people you know were not physically harmed, you have been emotionally and spiritually affected.

• What have you lost as a result of the natural disaster? If not totally lost, what has been negatively impacted or harmed? Your job? Special places in your community? Your feeling of safety and security? Your understanding of how the world works?

• Also consider not just what you have already lost but what perhaps you fear losing in the future. Are you afraid of future natural disasters and what might happen to you and those you care about? Are you anxious about future financial repercussions or other unknowns? Explore this idea as well.

CARPE DIEM
Write a list of all the things that you have lost or fear losing as a result of the natural disaster. Invite someone else affected by the disaster to do the same, then share your lists over coffee and conversation.

8.

BE AWARE OF THE RISKS

"There are wounds that never show on the body that are deeper and more hurtful than anything that bleeds."
— Laurell K. Hamilton

- For those most closely affected by the natural disaster, the psychological impact of the event can be serious and may linger for years.

- Natural disasters can be so traumatic to the human psyche that people who were formerly functioning well can begin to experience significant emotional and mental health problems. This does not happen to everyone, of course, but you should be aware that people who experience natural disaster trauma up close are more likely to divorce, suffer domestic abuse, commit suicide, abuse alcohol and drugs, and have economic problems. Keep in mind that these are risks—not certainties. Don't expect these things to happen to you or those you love. Simply be aware of the possibility.

- If you begin to notice such problems in yourself or others, take this as a sign that more help is needed. Don't shame yourself if this is the case. You have experienced a violent, traumatic event. Of course you need help! I am a trained therapist, but after our home burned down, I, too, needed to get support and counsel.

CARPE DIEM
If you are struggling or know someone who is, make an appointment with a counselor today.

9.

ALLOW YOURSELF A TIME OF LIMBO

"Limbo is the state where there are only questions."
— David Levithan

- After a natural disaster, many families are forced to live in limbo for weeks or months. Those who are displaced from their homes must find a new place to live and, at the same time, deal with the wreckage of their former homes. After our house fire, my family was displaced for 18 months.

- But even if your home was not destroyed, you have probably noticed that you and likely your whole community are feeling lost right now.

- It's normal to live in limbo for a time after a traumatic loss or experience. I also call it living in "liminal space."

- "Limina" is the Latin word for threshold, the space betwixt and between. When you are in liminal space, you are not busily and unthinkingly going about your daily life. Neither are you living from a place of assuredness about your relationships and beliefs. Instead, you are unsettled. Both your mindless daily routine and your core beliefs have been shaken, forcing you to reconsider who you are, why you're here, and what life means.

- It's uncomfortable being in liminal space, but that's where grief takes you. Without grief, you wouldn't go there. But it is only in liminal space that you can reconstruct your shattered worldview and re-emerge as the transformed you that is ready to live and love fully again.

CARPE DIEM

Even as you try to re-establish daily routines, you will still feel the unsettledness of liminal space after a natural disaster. Today, use a moment of your unsettledness to try something you've always wanted to try but never had the courage or opportunity to before.

10.

STAY IN TOUCH WITH YOUR FEELINGS

*"God created all of us to be emotional creatures,
and feelings are a big part of our lives."*
— Joyce Meyer

• You will probably feel many different feelings in the coming weeks
and months. You may feel, among other things, numb, angry, guilty,
afraid, confused, and, of course, deeply sad. Sometimes these feelings
follow each other within a short period of time, or they may occur
simultaneously.

• As strange as some of these emotions may seem to you, they are
normal. Your feelings are what they are. They are not right or wrong;
they simply are. Allow yourself to feel whatever it is you are feeling
without judging yourself.

• Stay in touch with your feelings by leaning into them when you are
ready. If you feel angry, for example, allow yourself to feel and think
through this anger. Don't suppress it or distract yourself from it.
Instead, acknowledge your feelings and give them voice. Tell a friend,
"I feel so mad today because…" or write in your journal, "I feel such
regret that…"

• Learning to name your feelings will help you tame them. As
Shakespeare's Macbeth reminded us, "Give sorrow words: the grief
that does not speak whispers the o'er-fraught heart, and bids it break."

• Don't self-treat difficult feelings in destructive ways. Alcohol abuse,
raging at those you love, not caring for yourself physically, and other
harmful behaviors are signs that you need more help.

CARPE DIEM
Using old magazines, clip images that capture the many feelings you've
been having since the natural disaster. Make a "feelings collage" on
poster board and display it somewhere you'll be able to reflect on it.

11.

UNDERSTAND THE SIX
NEEDS OF MOURNING

Need #1: Acknowledge the reality of what happened

*"Anything that's human is mentionable, and anything
that is mentionable can be more manageable. When we
can talk about our feelings, they become less overwhelming,
less upsetting, and less scary. The people we trust with that
important talk can help us know that we are not alone."*

— Fred Rogers

- When we experience something difficult in life, it can be tempting
to look away. "I am fine," we sometimes try to convince ourselves. "I
have it better than so many others."

- Yet no matter to what degree your family and your personal
belongings were physically affected by the natural disaster, you must
gently and in doses accept that you have been psychically injured.

- You will first acknowledge the reality of your grief with your head.
Only over time will you come to acknowledge it with your heart.

CARPE DIEM

Talk to someone else who experienced the natural disaster
in the manner you did. For example, if your house came
close to being flooded but didn't, find another person whose
home was at the perimeter of the flooding and strike up a
conversation with her. You will likely find that you share
similar thoughts and feelings about both the reality of what
happened and what could have happened but didn't.

12.

UNDERSTAND THE SIX
NEEDS OF MOURNING

Need #2: Let yourself feel the pain of your losses

"Face your life, its pain, its pleasure. Leave no path untaken."
— Neil Gaiman

• This need requires those who grieve to embrace the pain of their losses—something we naturally don't want to do. It is easier to deny, avoid, repress, or push away the pain of grief than it is to confront it.

• It is in embracing your grief, however, that you will learn to reconcile yourself to it.

• People with chronic pain are taught not to tighten around the pain but to relax and allow the pain to be present. When pain is resisted, it intensifies. You don't want to fight with your pain; you want to allow it into your soul in small doses so that eventually you can move from darkness into light.

CARPE DIEM

If you feel up to it, allow yourself a time for embracing pain today. Create your loss inventory (Idea 7) and dedicate 15 minutes today to thinking about and feeling these losses. Also, reach out to someone who is a good listener and explain your various feelings of loss to her.

13.

UNDERSTAND THE SIX
NEEDS OF MOURNING

Need #3: Participate in memorializing what was lost

"Farewell is said by the living, in life, every day. It is said with love and friendship, with the affirmation that the memories are lasting if the flesh is not."

— R.A. Salvatore

• Have you noticed that after a natural disaster, community members instinctively come together to pay tribute to what was lost? That's because as humans, we have a need to socially acknowledge and communally process events that affect the community.

• People leave token gifts, flowers, photos, and notes where lives were lost, creating a place for the community to gather and remember.

• Candle-lighting ceremonies spring up. Prayers are said, songs are sung, words of encouragement and community resolve are spoken.

• People gather in emergency shelters—some because they need food and a place to sleep, some to help, and others to simply be among people who are feeling what they feel and want to talk about what they want to talk about.

• When you participate in memorializing what was lost, your presence and story and listening ears not only help others, they help you.

CARPE DIEM
Find a way to participate today. Help a neighbor or volunteer at a shelter or write thank yous to emergency responders.

14.

UNDERSTAND THE SIX
NEEDS OF MOURNING

Need #4: Develop a new self-identity

*"People ... don't want to be cured or changed or eliminated.
They want to be whoever it is that they've come to be."*
— Andrew Solomon

• The fourth need of mourning involves developing a new self-identity. In the case of natural disaster grief, this often means coming to terms with the fact that you, your family, and your community are more vulnerable than you may have thought.

• "I never thought this would happen to me, my family, or my community," is a common thought after a natural disaster. Before the disaster, your self-identify may have been shaped in part by a sense of safety and permanence. Now you may feel unsettled, and may be considering relocating.

• You need to re-anchor yourself, to reconstruct your self-identity. This is arduous work. One of your biggest challenges may be to recreate yourself in the face of the loss of how you used to think the world worked. Let me assure you that you can and will do this.

• Many mourners discover that as they work on this need, they find some positive changes in their self-identities, such as becoming more caring, less judgmental, or less materialistic.

CARPE DIEM
Write out a response to this prompt: I used to think that
_____. Now that _____ happened, I have
come to realize that _____. This makes me feel
_____. Keep writing as long as you want.

15.

UNDERSTAND THE SIX
NEEDS OF MOURNING

Need #5: Search for meaning

*"In all natural disasters through time, man needs
to attach meaning to tragedy, no matter how
random and inexplicable the event is."*
— Nathaniel Philbrick

• When a natural disaster strikes, we naturally question the meaning
and purpose of life and death.

• "Why?" questions may surface uncontrollably and often precede
"How" questions. "Why did this happen?" comes before "How will I
pick up and go on?"

• You will probably question your philosophy of life and explore
religious and spiritual values as you work on this need.

• Remember that having faith or spirituality does not negate your
need to mourn: "Blessed are those who mourn for they shall be
comforted."

• Some people may tell you that asking "Why?" doesn't do you any
good. These people are usually unfamiliar with the experience
of traumatic grief. Try to reach out to people who can create a
supportive atmosphere for you right now.

CARPE DIEM

Write down a list of "why" questions that have surfaced for you since
the natural disaster. Find a friend or counselor who will explore these
questions with you without thinking she has to give you answers.

16.

UNDERSTAND THE SIX
NEEDS OF MOURNING

Need #6: Receive ongoing support from others

*"What is the appropriate behavior for a man or a
woman in the midst of this world, where each person is
clinging to his piece of debris? What's the proper salutation
between people as they pass each other in this flood?"*

— Buddha

- As mourners, we need the love and understanding of others if we are to heal.

- Don't feel ashamed by your dependence on others right now. Instead, revel in the knowledge that others care about you.

- Unfortunately, our society places too much value on "carrying on" and "doing well" after a loss. So, many mourners are abandoned by their friends and family soon after a loss or traumatic experience.

- One of the touchstones of grief is that each and every one of us as humans is connected by loss. As you experience the aftermath of a natural disaster, you are connected to every single person who has experienced or ever will experience a similar tragedy. As The Compassionate Friends (an international organization of bereaved parents) say, "We need not walk alone."

- Grief is a process, not an event, and you will need the continued support of your friends and family for weeks, months, and years.

CARPE DIEM
Sometimes your friends want to support you but don't know
how. Ask. Call your closest friend right now and tell her you
need her help through the coming weeks and months.

17.

BE AWARE THAT YOUR GRIEF AFFECTS YOUR BODY, HEART, MIND, SOCIAL SELF, AND SPIRIT

"She has been surprised by grief, its constancy, its immediacy, its unrelenting physical pain."

— Michelle Latiolais

• Grief is physically demanding. This is especially true with traumatic grief. Your body responds to the stress of the encounter, and the immune system can weaken. You may be more susceptible to illness. You may also feel lethargic, weak, or highly fatigued. You may not be sleeping well, and you may have no appetite. Your stomach may hurt. Your chest may ache.

• The emotional toll of grief is complex and painful. You may feel many different feelings that shift and blur over time.

• Bereavement naturally results in social discomfort. Friends and family who were not affected by the disaster may reach out to you initially but may soon withdraw, leaving you isolated and unsupported. There is truth in the saying, "You find out who your real friends are."

• Basically, your grief may affect every aspect of your life. Nothing may feel "normal" right now. If this is true for you, don't be alarmed. Just trust that if you continue to express your grief, over time you will find peace and comfort again.

CARPE DIEM

If you've felt physically affected by your grief, see a doctor this week. Sometimes it's comforting to receive a clean bill of health. Or, if you need some physical care, get it. Remember, your body is sometimes smarter than your head; it will let you know you have "special needs."

18.

TELL YOUR STORY

*"Something about telling that story made
my gut grow back together."*
— John Green

• The human brain needs repetition to develop understanding. That is why whenever you are learning something new, you have to study and repeat, study and repeat.

• When your brain is exposed to a natural disaster, it may repeatedly revisit the traumatic experience in an effort to understand. Flashbacks are common. Not being able to stop thinking about the trauma is common. This repetition is often unpleasant and can feel all-consuming.

• One way to begin to move the experience out of your RAM (your short-term, operational memory) and into your long-term memory is to talk about what happened. Articulating thoughts moves them from one part of your brain to another. This serves a physiological purpose. But it also serves an emotional and spiritual purpose because telling your story to someone who will listen and empathize activates your social support system. It's a win-win scenario.

• Telling your story one time will likely not be enough. If you continue to revisit it, that means you need to keep expressing it. It's as if each time you tell the story it becomes a little more understandable, a little more integrated into both your head and your heart. (But choose your listeners with care! See Idea 40.)

CARPE DIEM
Today, tell the story of your natural disaster experience. I encourage you to talk to someone who is a good listener face-to-face, but writing down the experience in detail will also help, as will sharing it online.

19.

LISTEN TO THE STORIES OF OTHERS

"Yes. We both have a bad feeling. Tonight we shall take our bad feelings and share them, and face them. We shall mourn. We shall drain the bitter dregs of mortality. Pain shared, my brother, is pain not doubled, but halved. No man is an island."

— Neil Gaiman

• Telling your natural disaster story will help your mind and soul acknowledge and process what happened. But listening to the stories of others will also help—because it will engage your heart.

• You've probably heard the ancient fable about the six blind men and the elephant. Each of them grabbed hold of a different part of the elephant, which caused a misunderstanding about what they were experiencing. The man who touched the trunk said an elephant was like a tree branch. The man who touched the tusk said an elephant was like a pipe. The man who touched the tail said an elephant was like a rope. In the end, the king explained to the men that each of them was right but that the elephant as a whole was comprised of all of these parts, and more.

• When you listen to the natural disaster stories of others, you begin to understand and embrace what the experience was like for people more broadly. This is not to diminish the importance of your personal story but to help place it into a context.

• Understanding that others, too, are experiencing shock, fear, anger, sadness, and the full gamut of thoughts and feelings will help you feel part of a community—a community in which individuals can help each other heal.

CARPE DIEM
Today, actively listen and empathize with at least one other person affected by this natural disaster.

20.

CONSIDER HUMANKIND'S STORIES OF DISASTER

*"Sometimes it can feel like the whole globe is spinning
with irredeemable losses, capricious natural disasters,
and crimes so outrageously evil they dismantle
any attempt to solve or explain them."*

— Karen Russell

• We humans have passed down natural disaster stories for millennia.

• The Biblical tale of Noah and the ark, for example, is a flood story.
When Mount Vesuvius erupted in the year 79 A.D., it led to the
most famous volcano story of all time: the destruction of Pompeii. In
contemporary times, we all remember the stories of the Indian Ocean
tsunami of 2004, Hurricane Katrina, and many others.

• Sometimes our stories tell us that God punishes us through natural
disasters (e.g., Noah and the flood). While I do not agree with this
interpretation, it's possible that, consciously or subconsciously, this
type of cultural or religious bias is complicating your grief. If so, I
suggest you talk to a friend or spiritual leader about it.

• Scientists think that natural disasters may grow more common and
violent as the world population increases (leading more people to
live in disaster-prone areas) and as climate change affects weather
patterns.

CARPE DIEM

Find a globe of the earth—not a flat map but a three-dimensional,
spherical globe—and hold it in your hands. Slowly examine
the continents and the bodies of water. Think about the natural
disasters you have heard about that have affected so many places.
Now find your home. Express aloud your hurt over the natural
disaster that has touched your community and your life.

21.

RE-ESTABLISH A ROUTINE

"I didn't want to fix it, to forget. It wasn't something that
was broken. It's just...something that happened. And like that
hole, I'm just finding ways, every day, of working around it.
Respecting and remembering and getting on at the same time."
— Sarah Dessen

• Depending on your proximity to the natural disaster, your everyday routine may well have been thrown out of whack. If your home was damaged or destroyed, this is certainly the case.

• But even if your home and your neighborhood are OK, the disaster has probably affected your routine in more subtle ways. Roads may still be closed. Power outages may linger. Parts of your community may be devastated. TV coverage and community conversations may still center on what happened.

• Our daily routines give us a sense of safety and control. If yours has been discombobulated by a natural disaster, try to return to it—or create a new one—as soon as possible.

• Getting up and going to bed at the same time each day, taking a walk or exercising at an appointed hour, having a cup of tea mid-afternoon, sitting down for dinner each night with your family— these are the kind of touch-points in your day that you can work to reestablish. Alone, none of these items are remarkable, but when assembled together to create the structure of your day, each becomes an important element in helping you feel safe and secure again.

CARPE DIEM
Write down the daily routine you hope to follow in the coming week. Make yourself reminders on your phone or in writing.

22.

EMBRACE THE UNIQUENESS
OF YOUR GRIEF

"Each of us has his own rhythm of suffering."
— Roland Barthes

• Your grief journey is unique. There is only one you. What helps others heal may or may not help you, and vice versa.

• I have explained to you the Six Reconciliation Needs of Mourning (Ideas 11-16), for these are the needs that all mourners must undertake to integrate an experience of loss into their hearts and souls. But I do not pretend to know all the intricacies of your grief; the Needs of Mourning alone will not define your journey.

• While in the aftermath of a shared significant experience mourners often have similar stories and circumstances, no two people grieve in the same way and in the same time. Comparing and judging your grief to another person's separates us on the path we all walk. This is not to say that you can't help each other; survivors of natural disaster often understand and empathize with one another in profoundly healing ways. Grief, while as unique as our individual fingerprints, is an experience all humans share.

• Just as you must accept the uniqueness of your own grief, you must also accept the grief responses of others mourning the same disaster. Accept these differences and do not judge others for their unique thoughts and feelings.

CARPE DIEM

Today, talk to someone else grieving this experience. Ask her how she's feeling and what she's been thinking about. Share your thoughts and feelings. You may be surprised at the both the differences and the similarities.

23.

DON'T FALL VICTIM TO THE CLICHÉ THAT TIME ALONE HEALS ALL WOUNDS

"It's time to live with what we have and mourn what we lost."
— Lev Grossman

- As a culture, we like to believe that we can and should avoid pain whenever possible. That's why we treasure the cliché that says, "Don't worry. As time passes, you'll feel better."

- One of the essential principles of grief and mourning, however, is that grief waits on welcome, not on time. In other words, grief must be experienced, even befriended, before it can soften.

- People who don't express their normal and necessary thoughts and feelings after a traumatic event end up "carrying" their grief. This means that they stuff it into a closet somewhere deep inside them and hope it never resurfaces. The problem is, carried grief results in problems with intimacy, relationships, anxiety, and other symptoms.

- Don't be a grief carrier. Choose to express your thoughts and feelings. It's the only way to go on to live and love fully again.

CARPE DIEM

Think of a loss in your past that perhaps you did not fully mourn. Is it still quite tender and painful to call to the surface? Do you tend to push aside any thoughts and feelings about this loss when they arise? If so, you, like many of us, are probably carrying some grief. You might want to explore your carried grief by seeing a counselor and/or by working with my book *Living in the Shadow of the Ghosts of Grief*.

24.

LET GO OF OTHER DESTRUCTIVE MYTHS ABOUT GRIEF AND MOURNING

"Beliefs have the power to create and the power to destroy. Human beings have the awesome ability to take any experience of their lives and create a meaning that disempowers them or one that can literally save their lives."

— Tony Robbins

- You have probably internalized many of our society's harmful myths about grief and mourning.

- Here are some to let go of:
  - I need to be strong and carry on.
  - Tears are a sign of weakness.
  - I need to get over my grief.
  - Death and loss and painful feelings are things we don't talk about.
  - I should try to put trauma behind me quickly and efficiently.
  - Other people need me, so I need to "hurry up" and get back to my "normal" self.

- Sometimes these myths will cause you to feel guilty about or ashamed of your true thoughts and feelings.

- Your grief is your grief. It's normal and necessary. Allow it to be what it is.

CARPE DIEM
Which grief myth has been most harmful to your grief journey? Consider the ways in which you can help teach others about these destructive myths.

25.

MAKE MOURNING A FAMILY AFFAIR

*"When everything goes to hell, the people who stand
by you without flinching—they are your family."*

— Jim Butcher

- If you are grieving in the aftermath of a natural disaster, understand that your family and friends, especially those who live with or near you, are probably also grieving too.

- Physical proximity to a natural disaster is just plain frightening and results in the kind of traumatic stress and grief we've been talking about.

- Don't assume that if your friends and family members seem "fine" on the outside that they're not grieving inside. If your thoughts and feelings about the natural disaster are bothering you, it's almost certain that others in your life are also troubled.

- Ask them. Talk to them. Initiate conversations about the natural disaster and invite them to open up.

- Bring up your own thoughts and feelings about the disaster in everyday conversation, such as at the dinner table or over the backyard fence. Informally talking through everyone's experiences in bits and pieces, a little at a time, may be just what is needed.

CARPE DIEM

Tell a family member or neighbor today how you're feeling
about the natural disaster. Ask him how he's feeling. Notice
if your feelings soften a bit after the conversation.

26.

UNDERSTAND THE PRESSURE COOKER PHENOMENON

"Be kind, for everyone you meet is fighting a harder battle."
— Plato

• Everyone who was affected by this natural disaster is grieving. Each and every one of these people needs and deserves the empathetic understanding and support of others.

• But wait...how can this work? Everyone needs help at the same time!

• When a community has been affected by a natural disaster, you'll see what I call the "pressure cooker phenomenon." Typically everyone has a high need to feel understood yet a low capacity to be understanding.

• If the pressure cooker phenomenon is making it hard for you to find someone who will listen to you without judging and without monopolizing the conversation with her own grief (though equal sharing of conversation time is appropriate), try turning to friends and family who live farther away. Online forums comprised of others who have experienced other natural disasters can also be helpful.

• If you are seeing the pressure cooker phenomenon within your own household, schedule a family meeting to talk about it.

CARPE DIEM
If you've ever used an old-fashioned pressure cooker (which is a kind of cooking pot where the lid clamps tight to the base, creating higher air pressure inside the pot), you know that there's a safety valve on the top that rocks back and forth to let off some steam. Without the safety valve, the pressure cooker would explode. Find a way today for you and your family to let off some steam.

27.

LIMIT YOUR MEDIA EXPOSURE

*"Those images help us understand the general
and specific magnitude of disaster caused by the
tsunami. The huge outpouring of aid would not
have happened without those images."*

— Bruce Jackson

• When a natural disaster affects you, your community, your region, your country, or even your world!, it can be tempting to follow every moment of the happenings on the internet or live TV.

• After all, today's technology allows us to "be right there" in a way that just wasn't possible for most of human history. It's horrifying... and fascinating.

• Staying informed is essential to keeping you and your family safe. But if gluing yourself to the TV is filling your mind and heart with images that keep you up at night, stop watching.

• Children, especially, need protection from too much and too graphic media coverage of natural disasters.

• Don't bury your head in the sand, but don't fill it with unnecessary fears and horrors either.

CARPE DIEM
Today, unless it's absolutely essential, take a break from reading
news stories and watching video coverage of the disaster.

28.

IF YOU'RE SUFFERING FROM AFAR...

*"I had seen people who had lost everything and everyone
they loved to war, famine, and natural disasters."*

— Chelsea Clinton

- You don't need to live in or near the disaster zone to be affected by a natural disaster.

- If you have close friends or family whose lives were touched by the disaster but you live elsewhere, it's normal for you to grieve for them. If your hometown or a place that was special to you has been devastated, it's natural for you to be devastated too.

- Many of us grieve major disasters throughout the world. The force of nature and its terrible, indiscriminate capacity to wipe away entire communities in moments shocks and saddens us all.

- If you're suffering from afar, most of the ideas in this book pertain to you as well. Grief is grief, no matter its proximity to the physical source. It's the strength of the emotional connection to people and places that causes it.

CARPE DIEM
If you're reading this book because you are grieving a natural disaster (or perhaps multiple natural disasters) that didn't affect you personally but had a devastating effect on your psyche, you also need to express your grief. Today, find at least one way to mourn. Tomorrow, find another. And so on.

29.

UNDERSTAND THAT THE DISASTER EXPERIENCE MAY COMPOUND PRE-EXISTING GRIEFS AND STRUGGLES

"The wind is scary...during a tornado or in life in general. You never know when a gust is going to come in your direction and change everything."
— David Walsh

• As human beings we are the sum total of our experiences. Before this natural disaster, you were living your life—a life that probably included both joy and pain. Now, to top it all off, you are having to cope with the aftermath of this natural disaster.

• Any challenges in your life that existed before the disaster may now seem harder. If someone you love died recently and now you have to cope with a natural disaster, it may all seem too much to bear.

• Pre-existing depression and other physical ailments, financial troubles, relationship issues—all of these struggles and more may worsen as a result of the natural disaster.

CARPE DIEM
If you were having a hard time coping with life before the natural disaster and now, after what happened, you feel like it's just all too much, I encourage you to make an appointment with a grief counselor today. Connecting with a compassionate companion who can help you through the coming weeks and months may be just the extra layer of support you need.

30.

TAKE CARE OF YOUR BODY

*"Keeping your body healthy is an expression of gratitude
to the whole cosmos—the trees, the clouds, everything."*
— Thich Nhat Hanh

• When we are under stress, our adrenal glands produce stress hormones such as adrenaline and cortisol. These hormones tell us that danger is near and prepare our bodies to run or protect us.

• The problem is that long after the event of the natural disaster, our minds may continue to ruminate on what happened during the disaster, which in turn continues to prompt our adrenal glands to release stress hormones. We feel "stressed out," and our bodies may experience digestive and sleep problems, weight gain, anxiety, and other uncomfortable symptoms.

• Because stress has such a physical component, it's essential to take good care of your body right now. In addition to using techniques that ease the mental stress, such as meditation, your body needs ample sleep, regular exercise, sufficient hydration, and good nutrition.

• Lay your body down for several 20-minute rest periods throughout the day. A daily 20 to 30 minute walk is also essential.

CARPE DIEM

Right this minute, or as soon as is practical, go for a short walk.
Start with five minutes if that's all you have the energy for. Add
one minute each day until you are walking a half hour each time.

31.

BE HONEST WITH THE CHILDREN

"Live so that when your children think of fairness,
caring, and integrity, they think of you."
— H. Jackson Brown, Jr

- Children are often forgotten mourners. We try to protect them from painful realities by not being open and honest with them. We hide our own grief because we don't want them to feel bad.

- But children can cope with what they know. They cannot cope with what they don't know or have never been told. When we're not honest with them, they typically imagine circumstances even worse than the truth of the people whose homes or lives were lost during the natural disaster.

- Children are amazing, resilient creatures. Tell them the truth. Use language they'll understand, but avoid euphemisms.

- Typically children require information in "doses." You may not need to explain every detail to them all at once. If you're open and loving with them, they'll come to you with questions as they're ready. Answer these questions honestly. In the long run, it's a mistake to hide even brutal truths.

- Model your own grief for the children in your life. It's OK to let them see you cry and get upset. If you're concerned that your grief is preventing you from caring for your children, ask relatives and friends to help take care of them right now.

CARPE DIEM

Tonight at bedtime, talk to your children about the natural disaster you are grieving. Ask them if they've been having any thoughts or feelings about it, then stop talking and just listen as you hold them close. If you don't have children at home but do have them in your life, use this same basic technique the next time you spend time with them.

32.

DRAW A "GRIEF MAP"

"Journal writing is a voyage to the interior."
— Christina Baldwin

- The natural disaster may well have stirred up all kinds of thoughts and feelings inside you. These thoughts and feelings may seem overwhelming or even "crazy."

- Rest assured that you're not crazy; you're grieving. Your thoughts and feelings—no matter how scary or strange they seem to you—are normal and necessary.

- Sometimes, corralling all your varied thoughts and feelings in one place can make them feel more manageable. You could write about them, but you can also draw them out in diagram form.

- Make a large circle at the center of your map and label it GRIEF. This circle represents your thoughts and feeling since the disaster. Now draw lines radiating out of this circle and label each line with a thought or feeling that has contributed to your grief. For example, you might write FEAR in a bubble at the end of one line. Next to the word fear, jot down notes about why you feel afraid.

- Your grief map needn't look pretty or follow any certain rules. The most important thing is the process of creating it. When you're finished, explain it to someone who cares about you.

CARPE DIEM

Stop by your local art supply or hobby shop today and pick up a large piece of poster board or banner paper. Set aside an hour or so to work on your grief map today.

33.

BUILD ON INTERNAL STRENGTHS

"You have to rely on whatever sparks you have inside."
— Lisa Kleypas

• What have you always been good at? Which personality traits and strengths have helped you (and helped you help others) during past challenges in life?

• Turn to those things now. If you're good at organizing, for example, help yourself and others affected by the disaster with organizational tasks. Perhaps they will reciprocate by helping you with something you're not so good at.

• Likewise, be on the watch for personality weaknesses and more negative tendencies that may derail you now. If you're prone to withdrawing, for example, ask the friend or family member you trust most to help keep you engaged socially, if only a little bit.

• Everyone is good at things. You just might need some prompting to recognize what those things are in yourself.

CARPE DIEM

Right now, make a list of things you are good at. The list can be a combination of personality traits, whimsical oddities, and practical tasks (like baking). Make it a point to DO at least one thing on the list today to help someone else affected by the disaster.

34.

GET HELP WITH FINANCIAL STRESSES

"A person is a person through other people."
— Lesotho Proverb

• Natural disasters often cause financial difficulties on top of the emotional and spiritual stresses. Home repairs can be very expensive. Lost work time, hotel bills, and travel costs can all contribute to financial overload.

• Even if you had good insurance, the paperwork involved in being reimbursed can be a tremendous burden, especially during this time when your brain may not be functioning well. If you are not a "detail person," be sure to get someone to assist you in this overwhelming process.

• If you or your family is under financial stress right now, ask for help. Ask someone you trust to take charge of your finances right now so you can concentrate on your grief. Call your consumer credit counseling agency. Consolidate your debts with a home equity loan. Talk to a FEMA representative about what resources are available to you.

• Whatever you do, don't ignore your finances right now. Delinquencies and defaulting on loans will only cause you bigger headaches in the months to come.

CARPE DIEM
Among your friends and family, who's the best financial manager you know? Ask this person to step in and help you with money issues for the next several months.

35.

LOOK INTO EMDR THERAPY

"At any given moment you have the power to say:
This is not how the story is going to end."

— Unknown

• EMDR, or Eye Movement Desensitization and Reprocessing, is an effective information processing therapy developed more than 25 years ago.

• EMDR therapy involves the talking through of negative events while using visual, auditory, or tactile back-and-forth, rhythmical stimulation. EMDR psychotherapists, who are specially trained, often use a machine that looks like a laptop. Some clients watch a green dot move side to side across the screen, some listen to a beeping tone that sounds in one ear then the other, some hold tactile paddles.

• While the client works through the traumatic event and its emotional paths, the bilateral stimulation helps dissipate its effects. Clients often report feeling "lighter" after a session. Trauma victims often say they feel "stuck." EMDR helps them become unstuck. It helps the brain heal by taking the negative emotional charge away.

• To find an EMDR therapist in your area, visit www.emdr.org.

CARPE DIEM

EMDR may be particularly effective for you if you have persistent thoughts and anxiety about the experience of the natural disaster itself. Just a few EMDR sessions may soften your intense thoughts and feelings. Make an appointment today.

36.

ATTEND A CEREMONY

"This is what rituals are for. We do spiritual ceremonies as human beings in order to create a safe resting place for our most complicated feelings of joy or trauma, so that we don't have to haul those feelings around with us forever, weighing us down. We all need such places of ritual safekeeping. And I do believe that if your culture or tradition doesn't have the specific ritual you are craving, then you are absolutely permitted to make up a ceremony of your own devising, fixing your own broken-down emotional systems with all the do-it-yourself resourcefulness of a generous plumber/poet."

— Elizabeth Gilbert

- When words are inadequate, turn to ceremony.

- Ceremony assists in acknowledging the reality, remembering those affected, offering support to one another, expressing our grief, and moving toward reconciliation and transcendence.

- Ceremonies that take place weeks, months, and years after a traumatic event can continue to be very meaningful.

- After a natural disaster, a public ceremony is often held on or near the site of the devastation. Attend this ceremony if you can. You can also create your own simple ceremony, as suggested below.

CARPE DIEM

Hold a candle-lighting ceremony. Invite a small group of friends. Form a circle around a center candle, with each person holding his or her own small candle. Have each person light his or her candle and share a thought or feeling about the experience of the natural disaster. At the end, play a song or read a poem or prayer.

37.

MAKE A CALL FOR HELP

"Love one another and help others to rise to the higher levels, simply by pouring out love. Love is infectious and the greatest healing energy."

— Sai Baba

- If you're struggling right now, this very minute, I recommend you call the Disaster Distress Helpline toll-free at 1-800-985-5990 or text TalkWithUs to 66746. (Spanish-speakers can text Hablanos to 66746.)

- Calls and texts are answered by trained, caring counselors from call centers located throughout the U.S. They are there 24/7 to help people who are suffering after any kind of disaster, whether caused by nature or humans.

- The Helpline is a program of the Substance Abuse and Mental Health Services Administration, or SAMHSA. You can also visit them online at disasterdistress.samhsa.gov.

- Canadian citizens can try Public Safety Canada at 1-800-830-3118.

CARPE DIEM
Call the Helpline or visit their website today.

38.

GUARD AGAINST SCAMS

*"Crooks move into disaster areas almost as quickly as
relief workers do… These scammers will run every
kind of rip-off, from conning people into signing
over emergency benefits to signing usurious loans to
fronting construction work that's never begun."*

— James Walsh

• Unfortunately, natural disasters provide an opportunity for scam artists. Whenever and wherever people are in crisis, scammers move in, taking advantage of people's vulnerability and need for immediate solutions.

• Scams add insult to injury, doing further harm to people who are already hurting.

• If you are among those who need help rebuilding a home or recovering possessions, make sure you are working with reputable companies. Call your local Better Business Bureau and ask their advice before signing any contracts or paying any money.

• If you are too emotionally stressed to make good decisions right now, ask someone you trust to help you. Appoint this person to communicate with and vet contractors, roof replacement companies, etc.

• Don't give money to a charity unless you are certain it is legitimate.

• After our house fire, we were approached by a number of people offering to help (attorneys, contractors, and others), only to discover their own self-interests superseded any desire to be of real help to us.

CARPE DIEM

Do you know someone else who might fall victim to a scam in
the aftermath of this natural disaster? Call him today and offer to
help him guard against being financially taken advantage of.

39.

SCHEDULE SOMETHING THAT GIVES YOU PLEASURE EACH AND EVERY DAY

"Find a place inside where there's joy, and
the joy will burn out the pain."
— Joseph Campbell

• Often, people who are grieving need something to look forward to, a reason to get out of bed in the morning. It's hard to look forward to each day when you know you will be experiencing pain and sadness.

• To counterbalance your normal and necessary mourning during this time of grief in the aftermath of a natural disaster, each and every day plan—in advance—something you enjoy.

• Choose something that you like to do. Now is a time for you to consider what makes you happy, what gives you joy. This is not being selfish, by the way. This is attending to your heart and soul.

• Reading, baking, going for a walk, having lunch with a friend, gardening, playing computer games—do whatever brings you enjoyment.

CARPE DIEM
What's on tap for today? Squeeze in something you
enjoy, no matter how hectic your schedule.

40.

REMEMBER THE RULE OF THIRDS

*"Toxic people will pollute everything around
them. Don't hesitate. Fumigate."*

— Mandy Hale

- I have discovered that, in general, you can take all the people in your life and divide them into thirds when it comes to grief support.

- One third of the people in your life will turn out to be neutral in response to your grief experience. They will neither help nor hinder you in your journey.

- Another third of the people in your life will turn out to be harmful to you in your efforts to integrate the grief and loss into your life. While they are usually not setting out to intentionally harm you, they will judge you, give you unsolicited advice about what you should do, minimize your experience, "buck you up," or in general just try to pull you off your path to eventual healing and transcendence.

- After our house fire, several people said to us, "What a great time for you to redecorate!" While these comments may have been well-intentioned, we didn't find them helpful.

- And the final third of people in your life will turn out to be truly supportive helpers. They will demonstrate a willingness to be taught by you and recognize that you are the expert of your experience, not them. They will be willing to be involved in your pain and suffering without feeling the need to take it away from you.

CARPE DIEM

Today, seek out at least one person who falls into the final third. She
will be your confidant and momentum-giver on your journey. Try to
avoid that second third, for they will trip you up and cause you to fall.

41.

TAKE IT SLOW

*"Life is like an ice-cream cone: you have
to lick it one day at a time."*
— Charles M. Schulz

• Natural disasters happen quickly. Healing in grief does not.

• Consider taking a one-day-at-a-time approach in the coming weeks
and months. Especially if you personally experienced the natural
disaster, your mind and your heart will need lots of time to embrace
the reality of what happened as well as all the thoughts and feelings
you will have about it.

• Don't set a timetable that dictates when you should be feeling better.
Grief is not predictable. It takes as long as it takes, and it often gets
worse before it gets better.

• There are no rewards for speed. Don't judge yourself or others for
how slowly you seem to be moving through your grief. In fact,
apparent speed may be a sign that grief is actually being denied or
bottled inside.

CARPE DIEM

Today, catch yourself in a moment of hurried activity. Stop, take a deep
breath, and force yourself to slow down and experience the moment.

42.

IF YOU FEEL AFRAID, FIND WAYS TO FEEL SAFER

"Natural disasters are terrifying—that loss of control, this feeling that something is just going to randomly end your life for absolutely no reason is terrifying. But, what scares me is the human reaction to it and how people behave when the rules of civility and society are obliterated."

— Eli Roth

- Fear is a very common emotion after a natural disaster. Our bodies are programmed to feel anxiety and fear in dangerous situations. Our natural "fight or flight" response helps protect us from harm.

- When others in our community (and even our world) have experienced the full force of a natural disaster and been injured or died as a result, we feel empathy. We imagine what it might have been like for them. We imagine what it might be like if the same thing were to happen to us. We imagine what it might be like if someone else close to us were to die in this way.

- While normal, these thoughts make you feel anxious and unsafe. You may have trouble getting through your day, sleeping, or going out in public.

- You can't begin to mourn and heal until you feel safe. Consider what would make you feel safer right now. Do you need to stay at someone else's house for a while? Would it help you to see a counselor to defuse your overwhelming fears? Would you like some extra help watching over your children?

CARPE DIEM
If you're feeling afraid—no matter how rational or irrational your fears might seem to you—talk about your fear with someone who makes you feel safe. You might find it helpful to talk to a professional counselor who specializes in trauma loss. Ask for help exploring your fears.

43.

IF YOU FEEL GUILT, EXPRESS IT

*"There's a resistance for people to talk about things
that make them feel guilty. When natural disasters
happen, it's easier not to feel guilty about it."*

— Walter Mosley

- Of course, happiness in the aftermath of a natural disaster is often accompanied by guilt. This is called "survivor guilt." Why did you and your home survive while others didn't? Why are you OK while others are suffering?

- Logically, we understand that our guilt doesn't make sense. It's not our fault that we were spared. It's not our fault that others were harmed.

- You may also feel guilty that you did or did not do something before, during, or after the natural disaster—something that ultimately had a negative effect on someone else.

- Like all other emotions, guilt is not right or wrong, it just is. Expressing it will help you work through it.

CARPE DIEM
If you feel guilty about anything having to do with the natural
disaster, talk to someone about your feelings today. You
might be surprised to learn that others feel the same way.

44.

IF YOU FEEL ANGER, EXPRESS IT

"When angry, count to four; when very angry, swear."
— Mark Twain

• Anger and other explosive emotions, such as hate and blame, are common after a natural disaster. Why would God indiscriminately destroy so many homes, so many lives, so many families? Why is life so full of pain and suffering? It's normal to feel mad about the unfairness of it all.

• You may also be angry at people whom you perceive acted badly or ineptly during the crisis. People who refused to evacuate, emergency responders who showed up too late, neighbors who neglected someone—it's normal and natural to feel anger toward others at a time of heightened emotions and consequences.

• At bottom, anger and other explosive emotions are a form of protest. You wish none of this had ever happened, and you are protesting the fact that it did. Behind the anger are feelings of fear and sorrow.

• If you feel angry, find appropriate ways to express your anger. Raging against others, harming others or property, and taking inappropriate risks and possibly harming yourself will help no one.

CARPE DIEM
Today, vent your anger by talking to someone about it
and/or by engaging in a vigorous physical activity.

45.

IF YOU FEEL SADNESS, EXPRESS IT

*"It's snowing still," said Eeyore gloomily. "However," he said,
brightening up a little, "we haven't had an earthquake lately."*
— A. A. Milne

- It's normal and necessary to feel sad after a natural disaster. People lost their homes! People lost their lives! Of course you feel sadness and despair.

- If you lost personal possessions that link you to your family history, it can be devastating. While some may say these things are just "material objects," they are so much more than that. Allow yourself to mourn their loss.

- If you personally know people who were affected by the disaster, you can act on your sadness by reaching out to help them. Don't wait for them to ask: be proactive and step in to do something that needs doing.

- If you don't personally know people who were affected by the disaster but instead feel a generalized sadness, you are experiencing empathy. Empathy is the human quality that allows us to put ourselves into others' shoes and to imagine what it must be like for them. You can put your empathy to good use by volunteering in your community or by helping a neighbor.

CARPE DIEM

Write a note today to someone who experienced a significant loss during the natural disaster. Even if you didn't personally know this person or family, jot down the thoughts and feelings you have been experiencing ever since you heard about this family's circumstances.

46.

IF YOU FEEL HAPPINESS, EXPRESS IT

"Eventually, all things merge into one, and a river runs through it. The river was cut by the world's great flood and runs over rocks from the basement of time. On some of the rocks are timeless raindrops. Under the rocks are the words, and some of the words are theirs. I am haunted by waters."

— Norman Maclean

- In the aftermath of a natural disaster, it's natural and common for people whose homes and loved ones escaped harm to feel relief and even euphoria.

- Whatever you are feeling, it's OK. Feelings aren't right or wrong, they just are. Expressing those feelings is what is important.

- If you feel happy, allow yourself to feel this feeling and have gratitude for it.

- Write notes of gratitude—to emergency responders who may have protected your loved ones and home, to God or your higher power for your ongoing life, to friends and neighbors who have been helpful during this time.

- Allow yourself a little celebration. Celebrating your good fortune is appropriate, even as you remember others who were not as lucky.

CARPE DIEM
If you experience moments of joy and happiness today, enjoy them. After all, isn't it wasteful to try to ignore or squelch delight?

47.

RELINQUISH CONTROL...

"This may sound trite, but bad things happen to good people, and when you're facing terrorism, natural disaster, you can have every wonderful plan in place, but I am a realist."

— Warren Rudman

• The awesome power of natural disasters makes us frighteningly aware that sometimes human beings have very little control over their lives.

• A basic principle of Buddhism is that life is difficult and unsatisfactory—but only because we fool ourselves into believing that the world is (or should be) predictable and stable. Buddhists believe that if we learn to relinquish control and accept that all of life is change, on the other hand, we can live in peace.

• As Mahatma Gandhi said, "Everyone has to find his peace from within. And peace, to be real, must be unaffected by outside circumstances."

• Now I realize that this is easier said than done! And I also am not suggesting that everyone must become a Buddhist. But I am suggesting that natural disasters teach us that we can and should learn to find peace and joy in the simple things of everyday life.

• Relinquishing control—to God, to the universe, to fate, or whatever you choose—will help you mourn well and go on to live and love well again.

CARPE DIEM

Find an affirmation on this subject that speaks to you and repeat it to yourself each morning when you wake up and each night before you fall asleep. Here's one I like: "I release. I surrender. I coast along with my hands off the controls."

48.

...BUT TAKE CONTROL OF
WHAT YOU CAN

"There are two big forces at work, external and internal.
We have very little control over external forces such as
tornadoes, earthquakes, floods, disasters, illness, and pain.
What really matters is the internal force. How do I respond
to those disasters? Over that I have complete control."

— Leo F. Buscaglia

- Yes, you must relinquish the idea that you can control your life. But at the same time, you can also embrace the reality that you do have control over some extremely important things.

- You have control over how you will respond to circumstances. You have control over how you spend your time. You have control over whom you spend your time with.

- You can choose peace. You can choose joy. You can choose love.

- While I took control of rebuilding my house after the fire, I also discovered I had to consciously build in time to grieve and mourn. I had to ride the rollercoaster of having some control while simultaneously surrendering to my lack of control.

- This is not to say that after a traumatic experience you won't need to grieve and mourn. Of course you will. That is my main point in this book! But with practice and over time, you can ultimately choose to experience life and all its ups and downs from a place of peace, joy, and love.

CARPE DIEM
Today, take control of your response to something that
happens. For example, if another driver cuts you off in
traffic, take a deep breath and send him a silent message of
blessing and forgiveness instead of reacting with anger.

49.

LEARN TO MEDITATE

*"Meditation is the tongue of the soul
and the language of our spirit."*
— Jeremy Taylor

• Meditation is simply quiet, relaxed contemplation.

• You needn't follow any particular rules or techniques. Simply find
a quiet place where you can think without distraction and rid your
mind of superficial thoughts and concerns.

• Relax your muscles and close your eyes if you'd like.

• Focus on your breath. When your mind starts thinking its monkey
thoughts, refocus on breathing in and out.

• Try meditating for 10-15 minutes each day. It may help center you
and provide a time of respite from your traumatic thoughts and
feelings.

CARPE DIEM
Try reflecting on this thought: "As I allow myself to mourn,
I create an opening in my heart. Releasing the tensions
of my natural disaster experience and surrendering to
the struggle means freeing myself to go forward."

50.

CREATE A MEMORY BOOK OR BOX

"Memory…is the diary that we all carry about with us."
— Oscar Wilde

• If your home and life were closely affected by this natural disaster, you may want to create a memory book of the event. After all, it is now part of your life story, and remembering the past is what makes hoping for the future possible.

• Assemble newspaper clippings, website printouts, photos, and other memorabilia of the disaster and paste them into a scrapbook or tuck them into a special keepsake box.

• Counterintuitively, you may find the process of creating the memory book healing. It may give you a sense of control and provide some order to an experience that was chaotic and out of control.

• You may also find the book helpful whenever you need to tell the story to someone new. Remember, telling and "owning" your story is essential to healing.

CARPE DIEM
Buy an appropriate scrapbook or keepsake box today. Don't forget to buy the associated materials you'll need, such as photo pages or photo corners, glue, scissors, etc.

51.

LEARN THE SCIENCE

*"Every great advance in science has issued
from a new audacity of imagination."*
— John Dewey

• While we cannot control nature, we have, in the last century, advanced science to better understand it.

• Learning about the science of the natural disaster that affected you may help you overcome some of your fear of it. I often say that we can't mourn what we don't know.

• Read up on the type of natural disaster you experienced. Attend a talk at your local library. Search on-demand TV programs about your topic.

• Learning more about the science might also include brushing up on the warning systems in place and the likelihood of your home community being affected again. You may be able to regain a feeling of security by linking into warning systems (such as ensuring you're on the reverse 911 list and signing up for National Weather Service alerts) or apps or by moving a little farther away from disaster's likely path.

CARPE DIEM

Today, learn more online about the kind of natural disaster that
touched your life. Nationalgeographic.com
has a good section on natural disasters.

52.

MARVEL AT CREATION

*"The meaning of life is contained in every single
expression of life. It is present in the infinity of forms
and phenomena that exist in all of creation."*

— Michael Jackson

- Our Earth is a marvelous, and sometimes terrible, home. How miraculous that this infinitesimally small, life-sustaining planet emerged in the infinity of space!

- Whether you are a follower of the Abrahamic religions of Judaism or Christianity or not, you may find the Biblical narrative of God's creation of heaven and earth (Genesis 1:1-6:8) soothing.

- Many other cultures and belief systems also have beautiful creation stories you can explore. Wikipedia's "List of creation myths" is a good place to start.

- Of course, the Big Bang theory of the universe's creation—science's answer to how our world was created—is also fascinating to learn about and ponder.

CARPE DIEM
Visit a farm, zoo, or aquarium. Consider the
wonder of your place in the circle of life.

53.

SPEND HEALING TIME IN NATURE

"I thank you God for this most amazing day, for the leaping greenly spirits of trees, and for the blue dream of sky and for everything which is natural, which is infinite, which is yes."

— e. e. cummings

• You recently experienced the destructive power of nature. Now may be a good time for you to experience the healing power of nature as well.

• Research shows that spending time in nature helps us de-stress. Natural environments promote calmness and a sense of well-being.

• Go for a walk or a hike somewhere beautiful near your home. Every five minutes, stop and spend a full minute observing. What do you see? Hear? Smell? Touch? Call on your senses to fully immerse yourself in this place.

• If you're the adventurous type, you might even consider camping or weekending in a remote cabin.

CARPE DIEM

Step outside and find a comfortable place to sit down. (If you live in a large city, you may need to walk to the nearest park.) Take a sketchpad or blank paper with you. Try sketching some element of what you see. Your artistic skill (or lack thereof) doesn't matter! What matters is paying attention.

54.

CONNECT ONLINE

"People are very reluctant to talk about their private lives, but then you go to the internet and they're much more open."
— Paulo Coelho

• In times of disaster, online forums can become gathering places for people to share information and, yes, mourn together.

• Has a Facebook page been created around this natural disaster? If so, you might want to spend some time reading through the posts and contributing one yourself.

• InciWeb is a government disaster information site where residents can find updates as the disaster is occurring.

• Disaster-specific websites spring up soon after an event has started and are usually maintained for the duration of the disaster and the recovery. Some of these sites allow comments and conversations, so they truly become virtual community gathering places.

CARPE DIEM

Do a search today and see if you can find an online forum for the disaster you are grieving. Read through the posts of others. See if your own thoughts and feelings are affirmed. Post something if you'd like.

55.

MAKE A SILK PURSE OUT OF A SOW'S EAR

"With the art therapy, as soon as they saw the paper
and crayons coming, we couldn't get it out fast enough.
And we told them to draw about the tsunami."

— Connie Sellecca

• Are you familiar with this expression? It means taking something bad or ugly and making it into something beautiful, useful, or valuable.

• Natural disasters create lots of waste materials—materials you and others can use to make things that are useful and beautiful.

• In the hands of skilled artists and artisans, demolition materials can be upcycled into furniture, sculpture, home decor, and more.

• Children grieving after a natural disaster will often spontaneously turn to art. They often draw pictures of their experience as well as play-act their understanding of what happened—in other words, they create theater!

• After a recent wildfire near my home, artists in the High Park Fire burn area created "Ashes to Art." Sixty different artists from thirty states created art that included ashes from the fire. The art was sold, and proceeds went to the local volunteer firefighting organization.

CARPE DIEM

Whether or not you think of yourself as artsy-fartsy, you might find it surprisingly healing to make art that captures your thoughts and feelings about the natural disaster. Make a plan to get together with a friend and spend an afternoon painting, making pottery, sculpting, or creating whatever sort of art tickles your fancy.

56.

SAVE UP FOR THE NEXT RAINY DAY

*"The big lesson I learned from Hurricane Katrina is
that we have to be thinking about the unthinkable
because sometimes the unthinkable happens."*

— Mike Leavitt

• This disaster may have depleted your emergency funds.

• Even if it didn't, maybe the devastation you witnessed around you
has made you a believer in the necessity of a rainy-day fund.

• Recovering a sense of safety and security is fundamental to your
healing. Restocking (or creating) an emergency fund will help with
this essential task.

• The house fire my family experienced made us realize the importance
of each moment while at the same time waking us up to the need to
maintain adequate emergency funds. I stopped working for several
months after our tragedy, and I am self-employed as an author/
educator.

CARPE DIEM

Create a savings plan that involves automatic deductions
or transfers. Knowing that you are contributing money
each week or month to your emergency fund—even if it's
just a few dollars—will make you feel a little safer, which
in turn will help you on your journey through grief.

57.

REASSESS YOUR INSURANCE

"Good luck is a residue of preparation."
— Jack Youngblood

• It's often not until a natural disaster affects us personally that we look carefully at our insurance coverage. And by then, it can be too late.

• Adequate insurance, like an emergency fund, is something that can help you feel more secure right now. And feeling secure is an essential step toward healing.

• Home insurance, life insurance, renter's insurance, car insurance, health insurance, long-term care insurance—they're all pieces of the modern-day financial puzzle. Few of us enjoy learning about and reviewing our insurance coverage, but boy are we glad we did when we need to submit a claim.

CARPE DIEM

Make an appointment with your insurance agent today. Discuss your concerns and fears with her. Understanding what is worrying you will help her craft insurance coverage that best meets your needs. While most of us hope and pray we never have to collect on insurance, when tragedy strikes we realize how invaluable it is.

58.

LEVERAGE TECHNOLOGY

"We cannot stop natural disasters, but we can arm ourselves with knowledge. So many lives wouldn't have to be lost if there was enough disaster preparedness."

— Petra Nemcova

- Technology can't yet stop a natural disaster, but it can help keep you and the people you love safe from one.

- Globally, early warning systems are now safeguarding the lives of millions of people who might have been injured or killed by tsunamis, flooding, and other natural disasters.

- Did you know that you can sign up to receive severe weather alerts via texts on your phone or e-mail? Go to www.weather.gov/subscribe to learn more.

- Many of us today have canceled our home phone service, opting instead to use only mobile phones. Look online or call your city and county offices to make sure your current phone numbers and e-mail addresses are in their emergency alert systems.

- For an elderly person who lives or spends a lot of time alone, a life alert system, which includes an emergency button worn around the neck, can provide additional peace of mind.

CARPE DIEM
Call your city and county emergency services office today (or visit them online) to ensure your current phone numbers and addresses are in their alert systems.

59.

LAUGH

"Through humor, you can soften some of the worst blows that life delivers. And once you find laughter, no matter how painful your situation might be, you can survive it."
— Bill Cosby

• Humor is one of the most healing gifts of humanity. Laughter restores hope and assists us in surviving the pain of grief.

• Don't fall into the trap of thinking that laughing and having fun are somehow a betrayal of those who are suffering after the natural disaster. Laughing doesn't mean you don't empathize with them. Laughing doesn't mean you aren't in mourning.

• You can only embrace the pain of your grief a little at a time, in doses. In between the doses, it's perfectly normal, even necessary, to love and laugh.

• I've heard it said that laughter is a form of internal jogging. Not only is it enjoyable, it is good for you. Studies show that smiling, laughing, and feeling good enhance your immune system and make you healthier. If you act happy, you may even begin to feel some happiness in your life again.

CARPE DIEM
Tonight, watch a funny movie together with someone who shares your sense of humor.

60.

CRY

*"Unless you have been very, very lucky, you have undoubtedly
experienced events in your life that have made you cry.
So unless you have been very, very lucky, you know that a
good, long session of weeping can often make you feel better,
even if your circumstances have not changed one bit."*

— Lemony Snicket

- Tears are a natural cleansing and healing mechanism. They rid your body of stress chemicals. It's OK to cry. In fact, it's good to cry when you feel like it. What's more, tears are a form of mourning. They are sacred!

- On the other hand, don't feel bad if you aren't crying a lot. Not everyone is a crier.

- If you are still in shock, you may not be able to cry even if you would like to. This is nature's way of protecting you at a time when you need and deserve to be protected.

- You may find that those around you are uncomfortable with your tears. As a society, we're often not so good at witnessing others in pain. Don't let those people take your grief away from you.

- Explain to your friends and family that you need to cry right now and that they can help by allowing you to.

- As a trauma survivor, you may even find yourself keening, which means a loud wailing or wordless crying out in lament at the devastation. Keening is an instinctive form of mourning. It gives voice to your profound pain at a time when words are inadequate.

CARPE DIEM

If you feel like it, have a good cry today. Find a safe place to
embrace your pain and cry as long and as hard as you want to.

61.

PRACTICE BREATHING IN AND OUT

"Life is full of beauty. Notice it. Notice the bumblebee, the small child, and the smiling faces. Smell the rain, and feel the wind. Live your life to the fullest potential, and fight for your dreams."
— Ashley Smith

- When your mind and heart are overwhelmed, your body reacts to the stress with shallow breathing, tensed muscles, and other uncomfortable responses. One way to relax your mind, heart, and body is to breathe mindfully.

- Autogenic breathing is fairly simple, yet effective. All you have to do is breathe in very deeply for four full seconds, and hold it for two seconds. Then slowly release your breath for four seconds, and hold for two additional seconds. Then repeat.

- You can do this any place, any time. The more frequently, the better. Try for a minimum of five minutes a couple of times each day. Odds are you will notice how calm and relaxed this makes you feel, both mentally and physically.

CARPE DIEM
Right now, set down this book and spend five minutes focusing on your breath. When your mind strays, which it will, don't get frustrated or angry; simply return your attention to your breath.

62.

ACCEPT THAT THERE MAY BE NO ANSWERS

"You can no more win a war that you can win an earthquake."

— Jeannette Rankin

- The fifth need of mourning (Idea 15) is to search for meaning in life and death. This is the natural process of seeking to understand why such horrible things happen, why people have to die, why you or others have been affected in this terrible way.

- The search for meaning can be a long and painful process, especially after a sudden, violent experience such as a natural disaster. How can one possibly find meaning in this tragedy?

- Many people touched by traumatic loss come to realize that there may be no meaning to the tragedy itself. No rhyme or reason. No great truth. No justice. But they also learn, over time, that there can be meaning in the ways we respond to what has happened.

- How can I help prevent this from harming people again? In what ways can I honor those who lost their lives or whose homes were destroyed? How can I become a more loving, compassionate, helpful person as a result of this tragedy? For many survivors of natural disaster, these are ultimately the questions that have answers. These are ultimately the questions that lead to peace and renewed love for life. While you may not be at this place right now in your journey, my hope for you is that peace does indeed come to you.

CARPE DIEM

Deep in your soul, what is the most troubling question you have about the disaster? Take a walk today and give yourself some time to consider your question and why it haunts you. When you're ready, you may want to find someone you can trust to explore this question with.

63.

START (OR RENEW) A DAILY
SPIRITUAL PRACTICE

*"Just as a candle cannot burn without fire, men
cannot live without a spiritual life."*
— Buddha

- Grief is a spiritual journey of the heart and soul. Your soul is the primary essence of your true nature, your spirit self, your life force— what I call your "divine spark." Your divine spark has been muted by your grief over the natural disaster, but it never goes out. Feed it as best you can, every day.

- One way to do this is to adopt a daily spiritual practice. For you, this could be praying each morning upon awakening or sitting in silence in nature each evening. Maybe it is more formal and involves going to a place of worship regularly and attending services and study groups. Or possibly it is informal, as in checking in with a best friend each night on how you are doing emotionally and spiritually.

- If you are unsure where to start, ask others about their spiritual practices. Spend time with people who embody the faith you wish to live.

- Your spiritual understanding is yours and yours alone, even if you adhere to a certain faith. How you commune with your spirit or feed your divine spark is uniquely yours to decide.

CARPE DIEM
Try a spiritual practice of your choosing today.
Spend at least five minutes on it.

64.

SLEEP

"Sleep is the best meditation."

— Dalai Lama

• Among the most common physical responses to loss are trouble sleeping and low energy. It is so common we even have a fancy term for it—the "lethargy of grief." You are probably finding that your normal sleep patterns have been thrown off. Perhaps you are having difficulty getting to sleep, but even more commonly, you may wake up too early and have trouble getting back to sleep.

• A normal night of sleep consists of several distinct stages and types of sleep. Stage 1 is the twilight zone between being awake and asleep. Stage 2 sleep brings larger brain waves, and we are no longer conscious of our surroundings. In Stages 3 and 4, our brains produce slower and larger waves, referred to as delta or slow-wave sleep. The "lethargy of grief" often results in sleep disturbance and the inability to get enough sleep in Stages 3 and 4.

• After about 90 minutes in the four stages of quiet sleep, the brain shifts into the more active stage characterized by rapid eye movement (REM). Brain waves during REM resemble those of waking, but the large muscles of the body cannot move. This is the time of vivid dreaming. During a typical night we spend about 25 percent of the time in REM sleep and may have four or five cycles of REM sleep. We need to have enough time in each stage of sleep for our bodies and minds to be renewed.

CARPE DIEM
Start tomorrow off better by allowing yourself to go to bed
at least eight hours before you need to get up tomorrow.
If you are having ongoing problems with insomnia,
schedule an appointment with your physician.

65.

REACH OUT AND TOUCH

"When I come home, my daughter will run to the door and give me a big hug, and everything that's happened that day just melts away."

— Hugh Jackman

• For many people, physical contact with another human being is healing. It has been recognized since ancient times as having transformative, healing powers.

• Have you hugged anyone lately? Held someone's hand? Put your arm around another human being?

• You probably know several people who enjoy hugging or physical touching. If you're comfortable with their touch, encourage it in the weeks and months to come.

• Hug someone you feel safe with. Kiss your children or a friend's baby. Walk arm in arm with a neighbor.

• You may want to listen to the song titled, "I Know What Love Is," by Don White. I have found this song helps me reflect on the power of touch. Listen to this song then drop me a note or e-mail (drwolfelt@ centerforloss.com) and let me know how it makes you think, and more important, feel.

CARPE DIEM
Try hugging your close friends and family members today, even if you usually don't. You just might like it!

66.

GO TO YOUR HAPPY PLACE

"Happiness is a form of courage."
— Holbrook Jackson

• When you find yourself anxious, an effective relaxation technique is to visualize a place that calms you and makes you happy.

• Your happy place can be somewhere you've actually been, or it can be somewhere you conjure in your imagination.

• Try to use all five of your senses as you place yourself in this calming environment. Imagine not only the sights but also the sounds, smells, textures, and tastes.

• As with anything new you try, it will take some practice for you to develop your ability to go to your happy place. Build your imaginary world a little bit at a time, detail by detail.

CARPE DIEM
Right now, close your eyes and visualize yourself in a place that soothes you. When you feel your mind straying to other thoughts, pull yourself back to this place. At first, see if you can spend one minute in this place. Over the course of weeks and months, see if you can work your way up to 10 or 15 minutes.

67.

LIVE IN THE NOW

"What day is it?"

"It's today," squeaked Piglet.

"My favorite day," said Pooh.

— A.A. Milne

- You may have heard it said that there is no past, there is no future, there is only this moment.

- In his bestselling book *The Power of Now*, Eckhart Tolle encourages us to truly be present in the current moment. "Life is now," he writes. "There was never a time when your life was not now, nor will there ever be... Nothing ever happened in the past; it happened in the Now. Nothing will ever happen in the future; it will happen in the Now."

- The challenge is that it is really hard to live in the moment. Our minds constantly revisit the past and think forward to the future. Our egos dwell on what was and what will be.

- The next time you find yourself ruminating about the natural disaster, consciously pull yourself to the present moment. Look— really look—at your surroundings. Take a deep breath and notice what you smell. Reach out to touch several different textures within arm's reach. Listen to the sounds you hear. Consider the power of now and revel in this moment.

CARPE DIEM

Right now, empty your mind of its concerns and just "be" in this moment. Breathe in, breathe out. Find at least one thing around you to marvel about or give thanks for.

68.

LOOK INTO SUPPORT GROUPS

*"Individual commitment to a group effort—
that is what makes a team work, a company
work, a society work, a civilization work."*
— Vince Lombardi

• Support groups are a healing, safe place for people who are grieving after a natural disaster to express their thoughts and feelings. Sharing similar experiences with others may help you feel like you're not alone, that you're not going crazy.

• Support groups give you a time and a place—as well as permission—to mourn. They can also give you perspective on the experiences, thoughts, and feelings of others. Finally, support groups provide you with ideas and choices for reconciling your grief.

• After a natural disaster, support groups sometimes informally spring up. Neighbors get together to chat. Friends meet for coffee. Make it a point to participate in these spontaneous opportunities to mourn and heal.

CARPE DIEM
Call around today for support group information. If you're feeling ready, plan to attend a meeting this week or next. Or call up a few others who have been affected by the natural disaster and invite them to get together for coffee and conversation.

69.

SEEK THE SUPPORT OF A COUNSELOR

"There are many ways of getting strong.
Sometimes talking is the best way."
— Andre Agassi

• While trauma and grief counseling are not for everyone, many mourners are helped through their grief journeys by a compassionate counselor. It's not indulgent or crazy to see a counselor after you are affected by a natural disaster—it's simply good self-care!

• If possible, find a counselor who has experience with trauma, grief, and loss issues.

• Ask your friends for referrals to a counselor they've been helped by.

• Your religious leader may also be a good person to talk to during this time, but only if she affirms your need to mourn and search for meaning.

CARPE DIEM
Schedule an initial interview with at least two counselors
so you can see whom you're most comfortable with.

70.

DON'T BE CAUGHT OFF GUARD BY "GRIEFBURSTS"

"The wave is the signature of every experience of life. By understanding the nature of waves and their characteristics, and applying that understanding to our lives, we can navigate life with a little more grace."
— Jeffrey R. Anderson

• Sometimes heightened periods of sadness may overwhelm you. These times can seem to come of out nowhere and can be frightening and painful.

• Even long after the natural disaster, something as simple as a sound, a smell, or a phrase can bring on a "griefburst." You may drive past a spot where someone was killed. You may come across a photo of the damage. You may see a weather forecast calling for severe weather. These experiences tend to trigger sudden, unexpected, and powerful waves of emotion.

• Anytime there are fire warnings or I see news of a house fire, I'm naturally brought back to my own experience. The powerful waves of emotion that come up demand my attention.

• Allow yourself to experience griefbursts without shame or self-judgment, no matter where and when they occur. If you would feel more comfortable, retreat to somewhere private when these strong feelings surface. Or, reach out to a friend who will honor your griefburst by listening and being supportive.

CARPE DIEM
Create an action plan for your next griefburst. For example, you might plan to drop whatever you are doing and go for a walk or record thoughts in your journal.

71.

WEAR OR DISPLAY A SYMBOL OF YOUR GRIEF

*"Never apologize for showing feelings. When
you do so, you apologize for the truth."*
— Benjamin Disraeli

• In centuries past, mourners identified themselves in some way to communicate that they were torn apart and in the process of grieving after a death. Wearing jewelry or wreaths made out of locks of hair of the person who died were common practices. Black clothing, or mourning clothes, was required to be worn for a period of one year. Sometimes mourners wore black armbands.

• These symbols of grief accorded a special status to mourners, saying, in effect, "Someone I love has died. Please offer me your respect and condolences."

• Today we no longer identify mourners in these ways, creating the harmful illusion that "everything is back to normal"—even though it's not and never will be.

• After a natural disaster, people sometimes place symbols in their front windows or on their car bumpers in memory of those who died or thanking emergency responders. Others wear buttons or t-shirts. People spontaneously create mourning symbols because they unite us in our grief and convey the essential message, "We have suffered a significant loss. Let's support one another."

CARPE DIEM
See if a symbol of this natural disaster has already been created.
If so, join in by wearing or displaying it. If not, maybe you could
work with a group of friends or neighbors to create one.

72.

WATCH FOR WARNING SIGNS

"I'd rather fight 100 structure fires than a wildfire. With a structure fire you know where your flames are, but in the woods it can move anywhere; it can come right up behind you."
— Tom Watson

- Sometimes in periods of stress and grief we fall back on self-destructive behaviors to get through this difficult time.

- Try to be honest with yourself about drug or alcohol abuse. Long after the event of the disaster, are you still taking drugs—prescription or otherwise—to make it through the day? Are you drinking in an attempt to dull the pain? If you're in over your head, ask someone for help.

- Keep in mind that trauma can actually change the biochemistry of the brain. You may very appropriately be taking some anti-depressant, anti-anxiety, or sleeping medications right now. And if you were taking medications before the natural disaster, you should continue doing so under your doctor's supervision. If you're forgetting to take your medication, ask someone to help you remember.

- Are you having suicidal thoughts and feelings? Are you isolating yourself too much? Talk to someone today.

CARPE DIEM
Acknowledging to ourselves that we have a problem may come too late. If someone suggests that you need help, consider yourself lucky to be so well-loved and get help immediately.

73.

MAKE SOMETHING WITH YOUR OWN TWO HANDS

"Write it. Shoot it. Publish it. Crochet it, sauté it, whatever. MAKE."
— Joss Whedon

• The act of making something yourself is an act of creation. Creation is the opposite of destruction and can help you regain feelings of control and power. Sharing your creation connects you with others, which promotes healing.

• Making art is a wonderful way to shape your thoughts and feelings into something tangible.

• Anything you make counts. Are you a baker? Bake cookies and give them to someone who is struggling with the effects of the natural disaster. Are you a piano player? Offer to play the piano somewhere your community gathers. Are you a gardener? Plant something in a pot and gift it to someone you care about.

• The quality of your creation is completely beside the point. Don't worry if your efforts are thoroughly amateurish. It's the process of making and sharing that matters.

CARPE DIEM
Make something today with your own two hands. Share it with someone else.

74.

PRAY

"A mighty fortress is our God, a bulwark never failing;
Our helper He amid the flood of mortal ills prevailing."
— Martin Luther

- Prayer is mourning because prayer means taking your feelings and articulating them to someone else. Even when you pray silently, you're forming words for your thoughts and feelings and you're offering up those words to a presence outside yourself.

- Someone wise once noted, "Our faith is capable of reaching the realm of mystery."

- Did you know that real medical studies have shown that prayer can actually help people heal?

- If you believe in a higher power, pray. Pray for the people who may have died in the disaster. Pray for your questions about life and death to be answered. Pray for the strength to embrace your pain and to go on to find continued meaning in life and living. Pray for others affected by this event.

- Many places of worship have prayer lists. Call yours and ask that your name be added to the prayer list. On worship days, the whole congregation will pray for you. Often many individuals will pray at home for those on the prayer list, as well.

CARPE DIEM
Bow your head right now and say a silent prayer. If you are out of practice, don't worry; just let your thoughts flow naturally.

75.

BE AWARE OF "GRIEF OVERLOAD"

"Man, when he does not grieve, hardly exists."
— Antonio Porchia

- Unfortunately, sometimes people (maybe you) experience more than one loss in a short period of time. The natural disaster may have resulted in many deaths or many homes destroyed. In your life, it may have been followed by an unrelated, unexpected death, or serious illness. Job loss, divorce, or another significant loss may have come on the heels of the disaster.

- When this happens, you may be at risk for "grief overload." Your ability to cope may be stretched beyond its limits. You may think of nothing but death, loss, and destruction. You may feel torn, grieving one loss this minute and another the next. You may feel like you're going crazy.

- Rest assured, you're not going crazy. You are, however, in need of special care. You must try to find ways to cope with all the stress yet still find the time and focus you need to grieve. Reach out to others for help. You cannot get through this alone. See a counselor, if only to help you survive the early weeks after the losses. Join a support group. Start a grief journal. Be proactive in getting help for yourself and mourning openly. Remember, you have special needs right now and deserve support.

- Fertile soil that produces healthy growth does so because it has been well-tended in the early cycles of the planting season. This is also true with our grief.

CARPE DIEM
If you're grief overloaded right now, sit down and make a list of five things you can do right now to help offload some of your stress. Make it a point to take action on these five things today.

76.

SAY NO

*"Grief drives men into habits of serious reflection,
sharpens the understanding, and softens the heart."*
— John Adams

• Especially soon after the disaster, you may lack the energy as well as the desire to participate in activities you used to find pleasurable.

• It's OK to say no when you're asked to help with a project or attend a party. You can't help others if you don't first help yourself—by giving yourself the time and self-care you need.

• You may have never learned to say no, but now you must. Perhaps you've seen the wonderful sign that says, "What part of NO do you not understand?" You need to learn how to say no to extra projects and social events and invitations that you don't have time or energy for. If anyone needs some quiet time right now, it's you!

• Realize that you can't keep saying no forever. There will always be that first wedding, christening, birthday party, etc. Don't miss out on life's most joyful celebrations.

CARPE DIEM
Say no to something today. Allow yourself not to feel guilty about it.

77.

GO SOMEWHERE DIFFERENT

"Sometimes it's a little better to travel than to arrive."
— Robert M. Pirsig

• If you are living in or near an area that was affected by a natural disaster, you might benefit from a short respite away from home.

• If finances restrict your travel options, you may still be able to get away. You don't need to travel to an island paradise (although if you can, I highly recommend it!) to be renewed. Staying with a friend or family member who lives a few hours away might be just the ticket.

• Escaping from the physical site of the disaster may help you regain your footing. You can't escape from your grief, but you can use a change of scenery to soothe your soul and take a short break from the devastation.

• When you're in the middle of chaos, it can feel like the whole world has gone crazy. Going somewhere more stable and serene for a few days may help you regain perspective.

CARPE DIEM

Today, make plans for a short respite away from home, even if it's only a day trip to a park or museum or a friend's home for a visit.

78.

LEARN SOMETHING NEW

*"You can learn new things at any time in your life if
you're willing to be a beginner. If you actually learn to like
being a beginner, the whole world opens up to you."*

— Barbara Sher

- Sometimes in the aftermath of a devastating event, we can feel stuck. We can feel depressed, and the daily routine of our lives can seem joyless.

- Perhaps you would enjoy learning something new or trying a new hobby. When you direct your mind through learning, you can feel some sense of control of your life. The trauma you are experiencing has ripped away your sense of control. Regain a little piece of it by learning something new.

- What have you always wanted to learn but have never tried? Playing the guitar? Woodworking? Speaking French?

- Consider physical activities. Learning to play golf or doing karate has the added benefit of exercise.

- The more you practice your new activity, the more masterful you become. Mastery is a form of control and power. Feeling powerful will help you in your journey through natural disaster grief.

CARPE DIEM
Get a hold of your local community calendar and sign up
for a class in something you have never tried before.

79.

ADVOCATE FOR SOMEONE ELSE

"Are you upset, little friend? Have you been lying awake worrying? Well, don't worry...I'm here. The flood waters will recede, the famine will end, the sun will shine tomorrow, and I will always be here to take care of you."

— Charlie Brown to Snoopy

- You are hurting. So are others. I am guessing that if you are reading this book, you are someone who has the capacity to take action and do. This means that you may be someone who is equipped to help others in need—others who may struggle with common tasks more than you do.

- Are there people whose lives were affected by this natural disaster who are not able to or good at advocating for themselves? Who might need assistance with paperwork or relocation or the activities of daily living? Maybe you can help.

- Ask around to figure out who needs help and how you could connect with that person or family. Local shelters, churches, and community centers are a good place to start.

- The act of advocacy is compassion in action. It makes a difference—both to those you help and to your own healing.

CARPE DIEM
Today, help someone else with something big or little that you are good at and they are not.

80.

TELL SOMEONE YOU LOVE THEM

*"Love is not the opposite of power. Love IS
power. Love is the strongest power there is."*
— Vironika Tugaleva

• This tragic experience has probably made you very aware of how love makes the world go 'round.

• Sometimes we love people so much, we forget to tell them "I love you." Or we (mistakenly) believe that they know they are loved, so we don't need to tell them.

• These three simple words have deep, spiritual meaning, yet we sometimes fail to see that until it's too late.

• My dad loved me, but it wasn't until just before his death that he whispered to me, "I love you." I miss you, Dad.

CARPE DIEM
Call someone you love right now and give them the
lasting gift of telling them you love them.

81.

TURN TO YOUR FAMILY

*"You don't choose your family. They are
God's gift to you, as you are to them."*
— Desmond Tutu

- In today's mobile, disconnected society, many people have lost touch with the gift of family. Your friends may come and go, but family, as they say, is forever.

- If you're emotionally close to members of your family, you're probably already reaching out to them for support. Allow them to be there for you. Let them in.

- If you're not emotionally close to your family, perhaps now is the time to open closed doors. Call a family member you haven't spoken to for a while. Hop in a car or on a plane and make a long overdue visit.

- Don't feel bad if you have to be the initiator; instead, expend your energy by writing that first letter or making that first phone call.

- On the other hand, you probably know some family members you should keep your distance from. They may be among the one-third who are bound to make you feel worse (see Idea 40). Remember, sometimes you can love someone even though you don't like them or feel you can count on them for support, compassion, and understanding.

CARPE DIEM
Call a family member you feel close to today.
Make plans to visit this person soon.

82.

GET A MASSAGE

"Massage therapy has been shown to relieve depression, especially in people who have chronic fatigue syndrome; other studies also suggest benefit for other populations."

— Andrew Weil

- The power of human touch shouldn't be underestimated. When we are touched in a loving or soothing way, our heart rate slows, our muscles relax, and our spirits breathe a sigh of relief.

- Getting a massage is a wonderful way to de-stress. You can go to a massage therapist, or you can trade massages with a friend.

- Massage therapists are trained in different kinds of massage techniques. The most common—the one you probably think of when you hear the word massage—is the Swedish massage, which is a whole-body therapeutic massage that relaxes the muscles and joints. Also popular are deep-tissue, shiatsu, hot stone, reflexology, and Thai massage.

- Just like exercise and eating right, massage is not a self-indulgence but rather an effective form of self-care. When you are grieving, excellent self-care is essential to your healing.

- Incidentally...several weeks after my house fire, I was on my way to get a massage when I got a speeding ticket. I was so distracted by my grief, I had no idea how fast I was going. Let me tell you, I needed a massage even more after that.

CARPE DIEM
Today, schedule a massage or ask a friend for a neck, shoulder, and backrub. See how you feel after.

83.

ORGANIZE A TREE PLANTING

"Trees are Earth's endless effort to speak
to the listening heaven."
— Rabindranath Tagore

• Trees represent the beauty, vibrancy, and continuity of life. They are also an amazing example of the good in nature.

• A specially planted and located tree can serve as a perennial memorial of the natural disaster. The tree is a symbolic, physical presence that helps represent lives that may have been lost and families whose lives were torn apart. When you visit the tree, it helps you memorialize what happened and convert your grief into mourning.

• You might write a short ceremony for the tree planting. (Or ask a friend to write one.) Consider a personalized metal marker or sign, too.

• With planning and permission, the tree could be planted in a public place, such as a park or open space, or you could plant one in your own yard, to serve as a reminder for you and your family.

• Consult your local nursery for an appropriate selection. Flowering trees are especially beautiful in the spring.

CARPE DIEM

Order a tree for your own yard and plant it in memory of those affected by the natural disaster. You'll probably need someone to help you prepare the hole and place the tree.

84.

LOOK TO THOSE WHO MODEL
HOPE AND HEALING

"Bad things do happen in the world, like war, natural disasters, disease. But out of those situations always arise stories of ordinary people doing extraordinary things."

— Daryn Kagan

• As I have said, you are not alone. While no one else feels and grieves exactly as you do over the myriad losses caused by this disaster, many others have experienced natural disasters and learned to live and love fully again.

• You may find it helpful to identify people who have not only survived an up-close, personal experience with a natural disaster, but who have learned to live more deeply as a result.

• Grief support groups may put you in touch with such people. You can also find many good books written by survivors.

• Your place of worship may offer opportunities for you to meet others affected by this disaster. You may want to look into support groups, lay ministries, and weekend retreats.

CARPE DIEM
Whom do you know who—despite adversity—exhibits the kind of love and hopefulness you'd like to regain? Contact this person and ask for his advice over lunch or coffee.

85.

GIVE TO THE CAUSE

*"I feel really proud that in the wake of such a
disaster that people are donating. They are going
to have such an impact on a lot of people."*

— Chris Doyle

- Financial giving is not only a way of supporting a cause, it's a way to affirm to yourself what you believe is important.

- "Putting your money where your mouth is" is a kind of ritual, really. It's a physical act that gives concrete, practical shape to your passions and values.

- How much you are able to give is less important than the act of giving. Every dollar makes a difference.

- Don't forget that in-kind donations are also helpful. Blood, especially, is always needed.

CARPE DIEM
Each year, the American Red Cross responds to about 70,000
natural and man-made disasters in the U.S., ranging from
fires to hurricanes, floods, earthquakes, tornadoes, hazardous
materials spills, transportation accidents, and explosions.
Consider visiting www.redcross.org to make a donation.

86.

VOLUNTEER

*"It shouldn't take a natural disaster to remind us
of the importance of service. It's something that we
need to incorporate in our daily lives, as a part of
our priorities of how we should live our lives."*

— Evan Bayh

- During and after a natural disaster, there are many opportunities to volunteer.

- Shelters need many hands. Neighborhoods need people to assist with clean-up. Families need places to stay and meals to eat.

- You can help. Take a look around and ask yourself, "Where am I needed? How is my heart calling me to help?"

- Volunteering is a form of mourning, you see. When you freely offer your time and talents, you take your inner thoughts and feelings and you express them through doing. Along the way, you are likely to talk to, listen to, and touch others about your experience and theirs.

- Do remember that you have to receive before you can give. If you try to volunteer too early in your own grief, you will actually hinder your own healing. So, while the time may come to for you to give through volunteerism, don't jump in too quickly, especially if you were personally affected by the disaster.

CARPE DIEM
If you are able, take a moment today to find a way, large
or small, to help. Notice how you feel afterward.

87.

LISTEN TO THE MUSIC

"Where words leave off, music begins."
— Heinrich Heine

• Music can be very healing when we are in grief because it helps us access our feelings, both happy and sad. Music can soothe the spirit and nurture the heart.

• Research shows that listening to soothing music can lower blood pressure, heart rate, and anxiety. Create a playlist of music you find relaxing and pleasant.

• Upbeat tunes can help you blow off steam. Play them loudly and dance. Sing at the top of your lungs!

• Do you play an instrument or sing? Allow yourself the time to try these activities again soon.

• Your community may hold concerts benefiting victims of the natural disaster. Attending these concerts is a wonderful way to feel your feelings, support one another, and contribute much-needed funding to help families and relief efforts.

CARPE DIEM
Research upcoming concerts or music shows in your area.
Make plans to attend one in the coming week.

88.

RECONSIDER WHERE YOU WANT TO LIVE

"Where we love is home—home that our feet may leave, but not our hearts."
— Oliver Wendell Holmes

- Some of us feel very connected to our hometowns and could never imagine living anywhere else. Others of us live where we live by default—because our parents lived there, because our jobs took us there, because a friend lived there long ago.

- If you could live anywhere in the world, where would that be? Why?

- If the place you live is prone to natural disasters (e.g., my home in the foothills of Colorado is in wildfire country), now might be a good time to consider moving somewhere safer as well as somewhere that best suits your lifestyle and realizes your dreams.

- My oldest daughter, Megan, went to university in Oklahoma City, Oklahoma. She spent many hours in basements waiting out tornadoes. While she liked the area in many ways, it became very clear to her that she would not be making Oklahoma City her permanent home.

- Don't make a quick decision if you don't have to. Instead, take plenty of time to consider whether you should stay put or relocate.

CARPE DIEM
Write a letter to yourself about where you would love to live and why. See what comes out.

89.

SIMPLIFY YOUR LIFE

"Our life is frittered away by detail. Simplify, simplify."
— Henry David Thoreau

• Many of us today are taking stock of what's really important in our lives and trying to discard the rest. A natural disaster can suddenly make it quite clear what matters and what doesn't.

• You may feel overwhelmed by all the tasks and commitments you have. If you can rid yourself of some of those extraneous burdens, you'll have more time for mourning and healing.

• What is it that is overburdening you right now? Have your name taken off junk mail lists, ignore your dirty house, stop attending any optional meetings you don't look forward to.

CARPE DIEM

Cancel your newspaper subscription(s) if you're depressed by the natural disaster coverage. Quit watching TV news for a while.

90.

PREPARE FOR ANOTHER DISASTER

*"Let our advance worrying become
advance thinking and planning."*
— Winston Churchill

• I certainly hope you never have to suffer through another disaster. But preparing for one "just in case" may help you regain a sense of safety and control.

• Buy or assemble two emergency kits—one for your home and one for your car. The one for your home can be larger and should contain canned food (protein bars are good) and water for your family for 72 hours, flashlights, extra batteries, candles, blankets, medical supplies, and whistles. The one for your car should contain as many of these items as you can fit as well as jumper cables.

• Create and review your emergency plan with your family. Where will you meet? Whose house could you go to if yours was in danger? Write each others' cell phone numbers down somewhere in case someone's cell phone isn't working and you can't access contact information.

• After you make these preparations, pat yourself on the back. You have done everything you can. Find a measure of peace in this.

CARPE DIEM
Look online for 72-hour survival kits or
begin to assemble your own today.

91.

INCLUDE CHILDREN IN PLANNING FOR THE FUTURE

"It is time for parents to teach young people early on that in diversity there is beauty and there is strength."

— Maya Angelou

• All of us who are affected by natural disaster feel a sense of helplessness. This is especially true for children.

• In the coming months and years, you can help the children in your life feel more in control of their destinies by including them in planning for the future. If you are considering a significant change, such as relocating, include them in conversations about the decision.

• Even if the changes you are considering are more minor, such as carpet and countertops in the rebuilding phase of your home, inviting children to participate in the decision making will help them feel more in control of their destinies.

• When children are helped to feel powerful, their self-esteem goes up and their sense of self-efficacy is heightened. These are traits that will help them with everything they do in life.

CARPE DIEM
Have a family meeting today. Ask everyone
to share what is on their minds.

92.

BE MINDFUL OF ANNIVERSARIES

"Grief is a process, not a state."
— Anne Grant

• The anniversary of the natural disaster may be an especially hard day for you.

• This is a date you may want to plan ahead for. Perhaps you could take a day off work on the anniversary.

• Plan to do something to acknowledge and mourn your grief on this day. Create a ritual for the day, something you plan to do every year on the anniversary. Your ritual could be as simple as taking a walk in nature or as elaborate as creating or attending a public ceremony.

• Reach out to others on these difficult days. Talk about your feelings with a close friend.

• I sometimes think of anniversaries as "honorversaries." This reminds me to give attention to, or honor, how the fire disaster impacted and changed my life.

CARPE DIEM
Make a plan right now for what you will do on the anniversary. Enlist a friend's help so you won't be alone.

93.

BE PATIENT WITH YOURSELF

"Even a happy life cannot be without a measure of darkness,
and the word happy would lose its meaning if it were
not balanced by sadness. It is far better to take things
as they come along with patience and equanimity."

— Carl Jung

- I'm sure you've realized by now that healing after a significant loss does not usually happen quickly. And because the grief caused by the natural disaster will never truly be "over," you are on a lifelong journey.

- In our hurry-up North American culture, patience can be especially hard to come by. We have all been conditioned to believe that if we want something, we should be able to get it instantly.

- Yet your grief will not heed anyone's timetable—even your own. Be patient with yourself. Be patient with those around you. You are doing the best you can, as are they.

- Practicing patience means relinquishing control. Just as you cannot truly control your life or nature, you cannot control your grief. Yes, you can set your intention to embrace your grief and take steps to mourn well, and these practices will certainly serve you well on your journey, but you cannot control the particulars of what life will continue to lay before you.

CARPE DIEM

When you are feeling impatient, silently repeat this phrase: "Let nothing disturb thee; Let nothing dismay thee; All thing pass; God never changes. Patience attains all that it strives for. He who has God finds he lacks nothing: God alone suffices." — St. Teresa of Avila

94.

COUNT YOUR BLESSINGS

*"Sometimes God will deliver you from the fire, and
other times God will make you fireproof."*
— Joel Osteen

• When you are faced with loss, it can be difficult to feel a sense of gratitude in your life, yet gratitude prepares you for the blessings that are yet to come.

• Many blessings may have already companioned you since your grief journey began. Somehow, and with grace, you have survived. Looking back, you may recognize the many supportive gestures, big and small, you were offered along the way.

• When you fill your life with gratitude, you invoke a self-fulfilling prophecy. What you expect to happen can happen. For example, if you don't expect anyone to support you in your grief, they often don't. By contrast, if you anticipate support and nurturance, you will indeed find it.

• Think of all you have to be thankful for. This is not to deny you your pain and the need to mourn. However, you are being self-compassionate when you consider the things that make your life worth living, too. Reflect on your possibilities for joy and love each day. Honor those possibilities and have gratitude for them. Be grateful for your physical health and your beautiful spirit. Be grateful for your family and friends and the concern of strangers. Above all, be grateful for this very moment. When you are grateful, you prepare the way for inner peace.

CARPE DIEM

Start keeping a gratitude journal. Each night before you
go to bed, recount your blessings from the day. At first
you may find this challenging, but as you continue this
daily practice, it will get easier and more joyful.

95.

WATCH FOR SIGNS OF NEW LIFE

*"Progress lies not in enhancing what is, but
in advancing toward what will be."*

— Khalil Gibran

- Natural disaster creates chaos and devastation. Where there was order and beauty is now wreckage and ugliness.

- But as time passes, the wreckage is cleaned up and order slowly gets restored. It is human nature to create order where there is disorder. And in natural settings, such as forests, new life pops up all on its own.

- Signs of beauty and new life begin to spring up. Surfaces are covered with fresh paint. Flowers are planted. Pretty new signs are hung. Native grasses and saplings emerge.

- Pay attention to and have gratitude for each sign of new life.

CARPE DIEM

Consider walking or driving through (or viewing online) the
natural disaster area now and then in the months and years
to come. Look for signs of renewal and ongoing life.

96.

REASSESS YOUR PRIORITIES

*"Things which matter most must never be at
the mercy of things which matter least."*
— Johann Wolfgang von Goethe

• Loss has a way of making us rethink our lives and the meaningfulness of the ways we spend them. The shock of a sudden, violent experience, especially, tends to awaken us to what is truly meaningful in life.

• What gives your life meaning? What doesn't? Take steps to spend more of your time on the former and less on the latter.

• Now may be the time to reconfigure your life. Choose a satisfying new career. Go back to school. Begin volunteering. Open yourself to potential new relationships. Help others in regular, ongoing ways. Move closer to your family.

• Many survivors of natural disaster have told me that they can no longer stand to be around people who seem shallow, egocentric, or mean-spirited. It's OK to let friendships wither with friends whom these adjectives now seem to describe. Instead, find ways to connect with people who share your new outlook on life.

CARPE DIEM
Make a list with two columns: What's important to me?
What's not? Brainstorm for at least 15 minutes.

97.

CONSIDER THE REST OF YOUR LIFE.

"It is not in the stars to hold our destiny but in ourselves."
— William Shakespeare

- Sudden, violent experiences often leave us feeling powerless. We were completely powerless to prevent the disaster; we were totally powerless in the face of the disaster; and we are now powerless to reverse it. But we can regain a feeling of power by deciding to take control of the rest of our lives.

- Will you merely exist for the remainder of your days, or will you choose to truly live?

- Many mourners take up a new life direction after a significant loss. Has the experience given you a new perspective on life? How can you choose to act on this new perspective?

- Sometimes choosing to live simply means living mindfully, with an appreciation for all that is good and beautiful and with a deep, abiding kindness to others.

- As a wise person once observed, "When old words die out on the tongue, new melodies spring forth from the heart."

CARPE DIEM

Do one small thing today that demonstrates
your desire to live over merely existing.

98.

UNDERSTAND THE CONCEPT OF "RECONCILIATION"

"Tragedy blows through your life like a tornado, uprooting everything, creating chaos. You wait for the dust to settle and then you choose. You can live in the wreckage and pretend it's still the mansion you remember, or you can crawl from the rubble and slowly rebuild."

— Veronica Mars

• Sometimes you'll hear about "recovering" from traumatic grief. This term is damaging because it implies that grief is an illness that must be cured. It also connotes a return to the way things were before the natural disaster.

• We don't recover from grief. We become "reconciled" to it. In other words, we learn to live with it and are forever changed by it.

• This does not mean a life of misery, however. We often not only heal but grow through grief. Of course we are never glad that the natural disaster happened, but our lives can potentially be deeper and more meaningful afterward.

• Reconciliation takes time, especially after a sudden, violent experience. You may not become truly reconciled to your loss for years, and even then will have griefbursts (see Idea 70) forever.

• Perhaps you have heard it said that healing in grief is a journey, not a destination. While you will never "arrive," do be sure to have others continue to walk with you on the journey.

CARPE DIEM
Think about the past losses in your life and the ways in which you've learned to reconcile yourself to them. Because it was traumatic, this experience may be harder for you to reconcile, but you can and you will.

99.

WATCH FOR SIGNS OF RECONCILIATION

"We are all wounded. But wounds are necessary for his healing light to enter into our beings. Without wounds and failure and frustrations and defeats, there will be no opening for his brilliance to trickle in and invade our lives. Failures in life are courses with very high tuition fees, so I don't cut classes and miss my lessons: on humility, on patience, on hope, on asking others for help, on listening to God, on trying again and again and again."

— Bo Sanchez

- As you embrace your grief and do the work of mourning, you will begin to notice
  - A return to stable eating and sleeping patterns.
  - A sense of release from the natural disaster experience.
  - The capacity to enjoy experiences in life.
  - The capacity to live a full life without guilt or low self-esteem.
  - The drive to organize and plan your life toward the future.
  - The serenity to become comfortable with the way things are rather than attempting to make things as they were.

- Reconciliation emerges much in the way grass grows. Usually we don't check our lawns daily to see if the grass is growing, but it does grow, and soon we come to realize it's time to mow the grass again. Likewise, we don't look at ourselves each day as mourners to see how we are healing. Yet we do come to realize, over the course of months and years, that we have come a long way.

CARPE DIEM

Consider whether you see any signs of reconciliation in yourself yet. If you don't, don't worry. If you are continuing to express your thoughts and feelings about the disaster, it will come. If you do, congratulations! You are healing your traumatic grief.

100.
STRIVE TO GROW THROUGH GRIEF

*"Someone who has experienced trauma also has gifts to offer
all of us—in their depth, their knowledge of our universal
vulnerability, and their experience of the power of compassion."*

— Sharon Salzberg

• Over time, you may find that you are growing emotionally and
spiritually as a result of your natural disaster experience. I understand
that you've paid a price for this growth and that you would rather the
natural disaster had never happened. Still, the experience may have
brought bittersweet gifts into your life that you would not otherwise
have.

• I had previously scheduled myself to write a book during the month
after my house fire. Much to my surprise, I discovered that that book
(*Eight Critical Questions for Mourners*) flew off my pen. I wrote the
book in one week! While I wouldn't suggest a house fire to inspire
writing, I discovered that the stress of the tragedy did in fact clarify
my thoughts and encourage my creativity.

• Many people emerge from the early months and years of traumatic
grief as stronger, more capable people. You may find that you're more
assertive and apt to say what you really believe and be who you really
are. You may no longer put up with baloney. You've already survived
something terrible, so anything still to come can't be so bad. And
you've learned what's truly important and what's not.

• What's more, many of you will discover depths of compassion
for others that you never knew you had. Many natural disaster
survivors grow to volunteer, undertake daily kindnesses, and become
more emotionally and spiritually tuned-in to others and more
interpersonally effective.

CARPE DIEM
Consider the ways in which you may be "growing through grief."

A FINAL WORD

*"Nature does not know extinction; all
it knows is transformation."*

— Wernher von Braun

Without a doubt, natural disasters are life changing. If your experience
was anything like mine, you are simply not the same person you were
before the tragedy. You have been through so much. How *could* you be
the same?

The Spanish author and philosopher Miguel de Unamuno y Jugo is best
known for a concept he called the "tragic sense of life." Boiled down,
his philosophy, which rings more and more true for me as I get older
and wiser, is that human life is just plain messy. It is not, nor has it ever
been, a straight line forward. It is marked by both loss and renewal,
disorganization and reorganization, and chaos and healing. Part of the
challenge of life is to find hope and joy while surrendering to these
contradictions.

Many people I have supported after a natural disaster have said to me,
"I have grown from this experience. I am a different and better person."
You are indeed different now. Your inner form has changed. Tragedy
often results in a humbled new understanding of ourselves, others, and
the world we live in.

But don't get me wrong. I understand that this growth came from
something you wish had never happened in the first place. Though the
grief and loss that result from natural disaster can indeed transform into
growth, neither you nor I would seek out the many losses of natural
disaster in an effort to experience growth.

Natural disasters create "legitimate suffering." My hope is that this
little book has helped you befriend your suffering in ways that create
momentum for you to come out of the dark and into the light.

My Prayer for You

May you continue to find hope for your healing, to live your life with a rekindled divine spark, to have meaning and purpose in your life and in each day.

No, you did not want this natural disaster to enter into your life. But it has come to you, and you have learned the importance of not only grieving your losses, but mourning them so that you may heal.

May you remember that while natural disasters happen quickly, your healing does not.

Be patient with yourself and befriend the mantra "There are no rewards for speed."

May you keep your heart open wide and be receptive to what life continues to bring you, both happy and sad.

And, in doing so, may you create a pathway to living your life fully and on purpose until you die.

May you live in the continued awareness that you are being cradled in love by a caring presence that never deserts you.

I sincerely hope we meet one day!

THE MOURNER'S CODE

Ten Self-Compassionate Principles

Your natural disaster grief experience is unique. While you must mourn—i.e., express your grief—in order to heal, there is no right way to grieve and mourn. The following list is intended both to empower you to heal and to help you decide how others can and cannot help. It is not to discourage you from reaching out to others for help, but rather to assist you in distinguishing useful responses from hurtful ones.

1. **You have the right to feel safe.** After a traumatic experience, it is natural to feel afraid. Until you feel safe, you will not be able to focus on embracing and expressing your grief. Do what you need to do to restore your sense of safety.

2. **You have the right to experience your own unique grief.** No one else will grieve this natural disaster exactly as you do. So, when you turn to others for help, don't allow them to tell you what you should or should not be thinking and feeling.

3. **You have the right to tell your story.** Talking about your feelings of loss and grief will help you heal. Seek out others who will allow you to tell your natural disaster story as much as you want, as often as you want. If at times you don't feel like talking, you also have the right to be silent.

4. **You have the right to feel a multitude of emotions.** Shock, numbness, fear, sadness, guilt, and relief are just a few of the emotions you might feel as part of your grief journey. Others may try to tell you that some feelings, such as anger, are wrong. Don't take these judgmental responses to heart. Instead, find listeners who will accept your feelings without condition.

5. **You have the right to respect your physical and emotional limits.** Your feelings of loss and sadness will probably leave you feeling fatigued. Respect what your body and mind are telling you. Get daily rest. Eat balanced meals. And don't allow others to push you into doing things you don't feel ready to do.

6. **You have the right to experience "griefbursts."** Sometimes, out of nowhere, a powerful surge of grief may overcome you. This can be frightening, but it is normal and natural. Find someone who understands and will let you talk it out.

7. **You have the right to use ritual and ceremony.** Attending ceremonies that memorialize people and places affected by a natural disaster helps you acknowledge and embrace the reality of the event. They also help surround you with the support of others who care. Participating in (or creating your own) rituals, even long after the disaster, is a way for you to mourn. If others tell you healing rituals such as these are silly or unnecessary, don't listen.

8. **You have the right to embrace your spirituality.** If faith is a part of your life, express it in ways that seem appropriate to you. Allow yourself to be around people who understand and support your spiritual beliefs. If you feel angry at God, find someone to talk with who won't be critical of your feelings of hurt and abandonment.

9. **You have the right to search for meaning.** You may find yourself asking, "Why did this disaster have to happen? Why here? Why now?" Some of your questions may have answers, but some may not. And watch out for the clichéd responses some people may give you. Comments like "It was God's will" or "Think of what you have to be thankful for" are not helpful and you do not have to accept them.

10. **You have the right to move toward your grief and heal.** While natural disasters happen quickly, reconciling your grief in the aftermath will not. Remember, grief is a process, not an event. Be patient and tolerant with yourself and avoid people who are impatient and intolerant with you. Neither you nor those around you must forget that experiencing a natural disaster changes your life forever.

WANTED:
YOUR IDEAS FOR HEALING
AFTER A DISASTER.

We'd love to hear your practical ideas for healing after a disaster strikes. We may use them in the next edition of this book. Please write and let us know about your experience with this book.

If an Idea is particularly helpful to you, let us know. Better yet, send us an Idea you have that you think other fellow mourners might find helpful. When you write to us, you are "helping us help others" and inspiring us to be more effective grief companions, authors, and educators.

Thank you for your help. Please write to us at:

Center for Loss and Life Transition
3735 Broken Bow Road
Fort Collins, CO 80526

Or e-mail us at DrWolfelt@centerforloss.com or go to this website, www.centerforloss.com.

My idea:

_____

_____

_____

_____

_____

My name and mailing address:

_____

_____

_____

ALSO BY ALAN WOLFELT

Living in the Shadow of the Ghosts of Grief
Step into the Light
Reconcile old losses and open the door to infinite joy and love

"Accumulated, unreconciled loss affects every aspect of our lives. Living in the Shadow is a beautifully written compass with the needle ever-pointing in the direction of hope."
— Greg Yoder, grief counselor

"So often we try to dance around our grief. This book offers the reader a safe place to do the healing work of "catch-up" mourning, opening the door to a life of freedom, authenticity and purpose."
— Kim Farris-Luke, bereavement coordinator

Are you depressed? Anxious? Angry? Do you have trouble with trust and intimacy? Do you feel a lack of meaning and purpose in your life? You may well be living in the shadow of the ghosts of grief.

When you suffer a loss of any kind—whether through abuse, divorce, job loss, the death of someone loved or other transitions, you naturally grieve inside. To heal your grief, you must express it. That is, you must mourn your grief. If you don't, you will carry your grief into your future, and it will undermine your happiness for the rest of your life.

This compassionate guide will help you learn to identify and mourn your carried grief so you can go on to live the joyful, whole life you deserve.

ISBN 978-1-879651-51-7 • 160 pages • softcover • $13.95

Companion
PRESS

All Dr. Wolfelt's publications can be ordered by mail from:
Companion Press
3735 Broken Bow Road
Fort Collins, CO 80526
(970) 226-6050
www.centerforloss.com

ALSO BY ALAN WOLFELT

Healing Your Traumatized Heart

100 Practical Ideas After Someone You Love Dies a Sudden, Violent Death

Death is never easy, but for families and friends affected by a sudden, violent death, grief is especially traumatic. Deaths caused by accidents, homicide, and suicide violate our moral, spiritual, and social codes. Things are not the same, nor will they ever be again. Persistent thoughts and feelings about what the death may have been like for the person who died—and what might have been done to prevent it—color the grief process. Strong feelings of anger and regret are common. Understanding and expressing these feelings helps survivors, over time and with the support of others, come to reconcile their loss.

Most books about trauma are written for mental health caregivers. This book is for you. It offers 100 practical ideas to help you through your traumatic loss. Some of the ideas explore the basic principles of traumatic grief and mourning. The remainder give practical, proactive suggestions for moving beyond the trauma and embracing your grief.

ISBN 978-1-879651-32-6 • 128 pages • softcover • $11.95

Companion
P R E S S

All Dr. Wolfelt's publications can be ordered by mail from:
Companion Press
3735 Broken Bow Road
Fort Collins, CO 80526
(970) 226-6050
www.centerforloss.com

ALSO BY ALAN WOLFELT

Understanding Your Grief

Ten Essential Touchstones for Finding Hope and Healing Your Heart

One of North America's leading grief educators, Dr. Alan Wolfelt has written many books about healing in grief. This book is his most comprehensive, covering the essential lessons that mourners have taught him in his three decades of working with the bereaved.

In compassionate, down-to-earth language, *Understanding Your Grief* describes ten touchstones—or trail markers—that are essential physical, emotional, cognitive, social, and spiritual signs for mourners to look for on their journey through grief.

The Ten Essential Touchstones:

1. Open to the presence of your loss.
2. Dispel misconceptions about grief.
3. Embrace the uniqueness of your grief.
4. Explore what you might experience.
5. Recognize you are not crazy.
6. Understand the six needs of mourning.
7. Nurture yourself.
8. Reach out for help.
9. Seek reconciliation, not resolution.
10. Appreciate your transformation.

Think of your grief as a wilderness—a vast, inhospitable forest. You must journey through this wilderness. To find your way out, you must become acquainted with its terrain and learn to follow the sometimes hard-to-find trail that leads to healing. In the wilderness of your grief, the touchstones are your trail markers. They are the signs that let you know you are on the right path. When you learn to identify and rely on the touchstones, you will find your way to hope and healing.

ISBN 978-1-879651-35-7 • 176 pages • softcover • $14.95

Companion
PRESS

All Dr. Wolfelt's publications can be ordered by mail from:
Companion Press
3735 Broken Bow Road
Fort Collins, CO 80526
(970) 226-6050
www.centerforloss.com

ALSO BY ALAN WOLFELT

The Understanding Your Grief Journal

Exploring the Ten Essential Touchstones

Writing can be a very effective form of mourning, or expressing your grief outside yourself. And it is through mourning that you heal in grief.

The Understanding Your Grief Journal is a companion workbook to Dr. Wolfelt's *Understanding Your Grief.* Designed to help mourners explore the many facets of their unique grief through journaling, this compassionate book interfaces with the ten essential touchstones. Throughout, journalers are asked specific questions about their own unique grief journeys as they relate to the touchstones and are provided with writing space for the many questions asked.

Purchased as a set together with *Understanding Your Grief,* this journal is a wonderful mourning tool and safe place for those in grief. It also makes an ideal grief support group workbook.

ISBN 978-1-879651-39-5 • 150 pages • softcover • $14.95

Companion

All Dr. Wolfelt's publications can be ordered by mail from:
Companion Press
3735 Broken Bow Road
Fort Collins, CO 80526
(970) 226-6050
www.centerforloss.com

ALSO BY ALAN WOLFELT

The Journey Through Grief

Reflections On Healing

Second Edition

This popular hardcover book makes a wonderful gift for those who grieve, helping them gently engage in the work of mourning. Comforting and nurturing, *The Journey Through Grief* doses mourners with the six needs of mourning, helping them soothe themselves at the same time it helps them heal.

Back by popular demand, we are now offering *The Journey Through Grief* again in hardcover. The hardcover version of this beautiful book makes a wonderful, healing gift for the newly bereaved.

This revised, second edition of *The Journey Through Grief* takes Dr. Wolfelt's popular book of reflections and adds space for guided journaling, asking readers thoughtful questions about their unique mourning needs and providing room to write responses.

The Journey Through Grief is organized around the six needs that all mourners must yield to—indeed embrace—if they are to go on to find continued meaning in life and living. Following a short explanation of each mourning need is a series of brief, spiritual passages that, when read slowly and reflectively, help mourners work through their unique thoughts and feelings. *The Journey Through Grief* is being used by many faith communities as part of their grief support programs.

ISBN 978-1-879651-11-1 • hardcover • 176 pages • $21.95

Companion
PRESS

All Dr. Wolfelt's publications can be ordered by mail from:
Companion Press
3735 Broken Bow Road
Fort Collins, CO 80526
(970) 226-6050
www.centerforloss.com

ALSO BY ALAN WOLFELT

The Depression of Grief

Coping with Your Sadness and Knowing When to Get Help

When someone you love dies, it's normal and necessary to grieve. Grief is the thoughts and feelings you have inside you, and sadness is often the most prominent and painful emotion. In other words, it's normal to be depressed after a loss. This compassionate guide will help you understand your natural depression, express it in ways that will help you heal, and know when you may be experiencing a more severe or clinical depression that would be eased by professional treatment. A section for caregivers that explores the new DSM-5 criteria for Major Depression is also included.

ISBN 978-1-61722-193-4 • 128 pages • softcover • $14.95

Companion
PRESS

All Dr. Wolfelt's publications can be ordered by mail from:
Companion Press
3735 Broken Bow Road
Fort Collins, CO 80526
(970) 226-6050
www.centerforloss.com

TRAINING AND SPEAKING ENGAGEMENTS

To contact Dr. Wolfelt about speaking engagements or training opportunities at his Center for Loss and Life Transition, email him at DrWolfelt@centerforloss.com.